Honoring the Child Spirit

Inspiration and Learning from Our Children

SHMULEY BOTEACH

in Conversation with

MICHAEL JACKSON

Vanguard Press
A Member of the Perseus Books Group

To Cheftziba, our baby and youngest,
our family's living embodiment of the childhood spirit—
for all the laughs, joy, and wonder you've brought to your
parents but especially to your eight elder siblings.
May the Lord shine His light upon you
and bring you peace.

Contents

———⟨⟨∞⟩⟩———

Contents

Introduction
Remembering Michael Jackson and His Childlike Wonder

———— ∞ ————

Children are G-d's gift to us.

A few months after Michael Jackson died on June 25, 2009, the *This Is It* documentary hit the theaters. It captured the preparations for the London concert series Michael was working on at the time of his death. Watching it with my wife, it solidified everything I thought about Michael's tragic death, specifically, that the world still refused to mourn him as a man and instead missed him as a performer. There were "Oohs" and "Ahhs" throughout the theater at the uncanny display of Michael's musical genius. "How could a fifty-year-old man still move like that?" "Look at how beautifully he sang 'Human Nature.'" People missed Michael's magic.

I didn't. I missed Michael's humanity. I missed a friend who had tragically died well before his time.

It remains a profound irony of my close friendship with Michael that I never really got to know him as Michael Jackson the superstar but only as Michael Jackson the man. I never saw him perform, declining even to accept his invitation to his Thirtieth Anniversary Concert at Madison Square Garden the night before 9/11. He never sang a single complete song for me. He never moonwalked for me and he never jumped up on his tiptoes and screamed "AAAUUUOOOO."

What he did do was bare his soul to me in the conversations we recorded over a two-year period for the express purpose of publishing them in an eventual book that would deal with his innermost feelings, especially the importance of children and honoring the childlike spirit within each of us.

But why me? Why did Michael select me to share with the public that part of him few had ever seen? Since the publication of *The Michael Jackson Tapes,* many have asked me this precise question. Why a rabbi and why a father of nine? I, who have nothing to do with the recording industry and barely even follow it—why would Michael think that I could understand him and what he was all about?

There are probably many answers to this question. There was the fact that Michael was a spiritual seeker and appreciated the long conversations we had on values, matters of the heart, and faith. There was the fact that I had written books on relationships and child rearing, subjects that deeply occupied Michael's thoughts. And there was the fact that as a rabbi I was immersed in biblical texts and scholarship, which had been so important to Michael in his Jehovah's Witness upbringing.

All these considerations played some role. But more than anything else, what connected me with Michael was my devotion to fatherhood and my wife, my commitment to having a large family, and my consecration of most of my professional calling as a writer, lecturer, and broadcaster to persuading parents to prioritize and appreciate their children.

I, like few others, could understand Michael's attachment to kids and why recapturing his lost childhood was so important to him.

Michael felt forever misunderstood by the public. He was a man of profound contradictions who almost forced people to choose sides. He was arguably the world's most recognizable face, yet also its most masked, both literally and figuratively. He was the world's best-known celebrity, yet he was enigmatic, reclusive, and mysterious. Onstage he exuded a boldness and confidence like no other, but in private he was painfully shy and deeply self-conscious.

In his regular daily routine of having three meals with his kids, reading them bedtime stories, following the news, and addressing recording and business concerns, his day could not have been more ordinary. Yet he was perceived by the public to be strange at best, a freak at worst. He appreciated children more than any other global personality, yet his motives for doing so aroused grave suspicions among his detractors.

Aware of the public's perception of these deep contradictions and aware of how harshly people judged him without even knowing him, Michael began to close himself off from the world. As the years went by he became more reclusive, choosing to spend more and more time isolated in the expansive acreage of Neverland, the fantasy ranch and playland he created in the hills near Santa Barbara, than he did with friends or even family.

But Michael found me a little different from the average person he met. First, I was a man who lived many of the same contradictions that he did, something he commented on almost immediately. I was a rabbi steeped in religion, but I used every modern means available to communicate a spiritual message. I was a traditionalist who championed the family and marriage but wrote books on married couples having the most passionate and intimate sexual union. I believed in strict discipline in raising children but believed even more in raising children who expressed their innately bold, individualistic, and charismatic personalities. And while I revolved in media circles, I brought my children with me wherever I traveled because, however many comments it elicited, they were my real joy.

As we connected through the web of these contradictions, Michael came to feel not only that I shared his love of parenting but that, like him, I believed that children could heal the cynicism and stuffiness of the adult world, that there was no cure greater for cynical moms and dads who had lost some of their zest for life than to get on the floor near a fireplace and read their children exciting bedtime stories. Many times, we agreed that the pain and brokenness that are so often characteristic of adult life, born of vanished dreams and deep disappointments, could be dissipated through exposure to the loving and creative children in our lives.

When Michael and I met, I had seven children. I spent huge amounts of time with my kids and considered my interactions with them to be the single greatest learning experience of my life. From my children I learned innocence, playfulness, and acceptance. I learned to forgive quickly and to be awed by things like trees, pictures, and frogs. And I learned to treat everybody equally rather than create a hierarchy of the more important and the less so. I spent a lot of time with my children not because I was a great dad but because I enjoyed it. It involved no sacrifice at all.

I had had a displaced and unhappy childhood myself, and I had vowed to give my children the peace and stability that my own upbringing lacked. My parents, though exceptionally devoted to their children, had fought a great deal, divorced when I was eight, and thereafter lived 3,000 miles away from each other. Our family had come completely apart.

With all these very basic human commonalities, albeit on different scales, and with our ongoing friendship and conversations about life's experiences deepening, Michael did something he probably had never done before: He brought me into the mental universe he inhabited with children. It was a private place where no adults were allowed—a place only men and women who indulged their own inner child could ever understand.

In the course of our conversations, Michael began to share with me the endless lessons he learned from the time he spent with children. He revealed to me his adamant belief that the childhood curiosity he so steadfastly held on to was the source of his limitless professional creativity. He attributed his astonishing success to his refusal to fully grow into the narrow and defined mental world of adults.

For Michael, the child's world was one of purity, artistry, openness, and acceptance. Adults were doubters, but children had a natural capacity to believe. Adults were boring monoliths, usually interested in one-dimensional obsessions like money and social status. But children were natural polymaths, interested in the full color of the rainbow. The adult's world was one of corruption, calcification, and competitiveness. But the child's world was innocent and free. There was so much to weigh you down in the world of the adult. But in a child's world, you could soar.

It has long been said by armchair Michael Jackson analysts that Michael was a victim of arrested development. I disagree. I believe Michael *consciously* chose not to grow up. There was nothing arrested about it. He could, when he chose to, compete and thrive in the world of adults and usually beat them at their own pastimes. I have a video of Michael pitching a group of Wall Street investment bankers on his idea of transforming

Neverland into a water theme park. The presentation could compete with that of many a CEO. He certainly earned a top slot in the money-and-fame game.

Even though Michael was prepared to make forays into the world of adults, he refused to reside there. He felt compromised. Around adults who constantly scrutinized him, he could never be his truest self. Had he allowed himself to grow up fully, he would, in his opinion, have lost his creativity, stopped being innocent, and ceased having fun. So, like a snorkeler who will occasionally penetrate the ocean's depths, Michael poked around in the adult world. But he had to come back up because it was a world that he found suffocating.

This is what makes this second book derived from the tapes we recorded so fascinating. It focuses almost exclusively on Michael's insights into the world of children. In these pages—which have been arranged to capture the themes of childlike values that were so central to his being—we have Michael's core. We hear in his own words the song of his soul and we glimpse his irreducible essence.

Michael spent an enormous amount of time delving into the mental world of a child. As he ceaselessly explored its terrain, he became insightful about the essential childlike qualities that make children so imaginative, so creative, and so inspiring. No doubt you will find these insights as moving as I did.

There was, of course, a dark side. The man who made the insights contained in this book was the very same man who was accused of serious transgressions against children.

In my opinion, no matter what the final cause of Michael's death, there can be no doubt that Michael Jackson died of a broken heart, of deep and lasting pain, and that the principal twin causes of that pain were a broken relationship with his own father and the fact that innumerable people believed that he was a predator who preyed on unsuspecting children. In many television interviews in which Michael discussed the accusations against him, he denied being "Jack the Ripper," an epithet he brought up on many occasions. Michael knew that some people put his interest in children in the same category as the famous murderer's interest in women. It was excruciating for Michael that the area of his life that meant the most to him, the one to which he yearned to contribute most, became the aspect of his life that engendered so much hatred.

Michael delved into the world of the child in order to capture something of its preciousness so that he might experience all that he had been denied as a child performer. He also wanted to use his insights about children to inspire adults to be more innocent, more nurturing, more childlike. He wanted parents to put their children first, and he spoke to me often of his dream of establishing an international children's day, on which parents would spend an entire, uninterrupted day with their kids. But his detractors turned this all on its head. They saw Michael's expressed interest in kids as a thin veneer masking the classic signs of a pedophile. To a great extent, Michael never healed from the 1993 molestation allegations against him. And though found innocent, he certainly never fully recovered from his 2003 arrest.

Perhaps this was another reason that Michael chose me to finally liberate his insights about children. He knew that I did not believe the allegations. He felt I had come to know his heart, to know that he could not harm a child. And truth be told, years have passed and even after roundly and publicly criticizing Michael's admission to having shared a bed with a child not his own as utterly unacceptable and immoral—which it was—I still do not believe that Michael Jackson ever did, or could, molest a child. I believe the allegations are false.

Michael knew that because I was prepared to be critical of him for other aspects of his life—which I was, and with some frequency—the fact that I believed him on the molestation allegations meant something very important. I, who was one of the few and perhaps the only person in Michael's life who constantly lectured him about how he had to make major changes in his life to reverse his central decline, believed him on the subject that meant the most to him.

I was not a blind fan who saw no wrong in Michael. I told him endlessly that his plastic surgery was disfiguring him, that his prescription drug habit was killing him, and that his reclusive lifestyle was making his heart shrivel. He listened patiently until, after two years, he could listen no more and our relationship began to weaken. But this did mean that when I showed him real appreciation for caring about kids and for demonstrating to the world that its biggest star wanted nothing more than to highlight the plight of the world's children, my appreciation was sincere and genuine.

I recognize that a book based on Michael Jackson's insights into childhood will puzzle some, infuriate many, and be readily dismissed by others. For Michael's fans, their idol can do no wrong. But for Michael's detractors, the beast can do no right.

For the many skeptics out there—and I respect your right to be skeptical—I offer a famous Jewish teaching, articulated by one of Judaism's greatest thinkers, the medieval sage Maimonides, by which I have endeavored to live my life: Embrace the truth regardless of its source.

This axiom not only means the obvious, that we have something to learn from everyone. Rather, its particular application is most apt when there may be some hesitation to learn something from someone who appears morally ambiguous. Try your best to learn good things from them, even as you dismiss the items you disagree with or even deplore. May I remind you that Michael was never arrested in 1993, when the first allegations surfaced, and that substantial and credible doubts about the motives of the father of Michael's accuser have been raised? May I also remind you, as I just stated above, that Michael was unanimously acquitted on the other charges of child molestation in 2005?

So why would we close our minds and hearts to learning about the preciousness of a child from a world-renowned performer who was always honest about how damaged he was by having been denied a childhood? Michael believed that parents had a lot more to learn from their children than children from their parents. He also believed, as do I, that parents need their children even more than children need their parents.

This is especially true in an age where kids are being greatly devalued. Many parents today are workaholics who don't spend quantity or quality time with their kids. Others come home at decent hours, only to plunk themselves in front of the TV and ignore their children for the rest of the evening. Michael and his children spent many Friday night Sabbath dinners together with my family at our home. And it was, in part, because of the special time we spent together, as well as Michael's wish to establish some sort of international children's day, on which parents would put their kids first, that I launched a program called Turn Friday Night into Family Night, designed to create an international weekly family dinner night when parents would give their children the "Triple Two." Two uninterrupted hours, with two invited guests, discussing two important subjects. Why is this so important? Because only around 30 percent of American families sit down for dinner together on a regular basis. We parents are simply failing to put our kids first and make them feel special. Is it any surprise, therefore, that more than anything else, today's kids want to be famous? They seek to compensate for the lack of love with an abundance of attention.

Childhood has been so cheapened that children don't even want to be kids anymore. In our media- and technology-filled world, they absorb an overwhelming amount of words, images, music, and beliefs that aren't very valuable or substantive. Worse, the culture into which they are immersed hardly protects or preserves childlike innocence and youthful wonder.

In an age when families are fragmented and children are hell-bent on rushing to some I'm-all-grown-up finish line, is Michael's call for rediscovering the magic of childhood not somewhat welcome? Should we not try to slow down our children's headlong striving for adulthood by convincing them that childhood is the most precious stage of their lives and that homes built on skimpy foundations end up rickety and unsound?

As Michael and I recorded the interviews for this book, I found myself thinking deeply into the conversations. Imagine it. Two adult men, both dads, sitting for several hours together at a stretch in venues as distant as California and London, talking about what? Not Wall Street and how to make money. Not football and whose team would win the Super Bowl. Not politics and who would be the next president. But about kids. Their kids, the world's kids. Talking about how much more beautiful the world would be, how much more pleasant life might be, if adults unearthed their buried inner child. If they took the mothballs off childhood wonder. If they took the restraints off effusive displays of emotion. And if they brought the fresh air of childlike curiosity to the dusty cellars of adult pessimism. What a wonderful world it would be.

Soon our conversations came around to identifying the essential childlike qualities that adults should strive to retain. Things like joy, passion, inquisitiveness, the ability to marvel, playfulness, seeing with the mind's eye, forgiveness, and a lack of shame in demonstrating ignorance and asking questions in order to know. The more we spoke, the more I felt those child-like qualities bubbling up inside. At times I even saw things from Michael's perspective. I would finish a conversation, then go back to the adult world I inhabited, and it seemed a lot less impressive than it had a few hours before.

Michael believed that adults spend most of their lives trying to impress each other instead of just being natural. And they're always angling for financial or political advantage. They slowly come to see interactions with other humans as means to their ends. Michael constantly told me how much he disliked people befriending him because he was famous. He loved being around kids because they had no agenda. Likewise, I began to see that many people don't have friendships so much as con-tacts. Men and women who say one thing mean something else entirely. And people's egos get in the way of the selfless lives they really wish to live.

As Michael and I spoke, I sometimes felt transported to a far more innocent place, where things as simple as clouds were endlessly fascinating and flowers were more impressive than Ferraris. It may all sound corny now, but that is how I felt. And looking back, I miss these conversations because they helped me appreciate my children much more.

When I came home to my kids after many of these conversations—and it often entailed flying home to New Jersey from Neverland—I found myself enjoying my kids more deeply. I was more patient with them. I listened more intently to what they had to say. I was already an involved father. But was my involvement on my terms, or on theirs? Did I expect them to join me in the world of adult maturity and responsibility, forever admonishing them for irresponsible, childish behavior, or was I allowing myself to be dragged into their world of light-heartedness and joy?

I began to slowly surrender my long-held belief that sculpting and chiseling my children into an image I deigned worthy was the best form of parenting. It was now my dedication to understanding and knowing them that was so important. I had to learn to parent them, as King Solomon says in Proverbs, "according to *their* way." I was now seeing things from Michael's perspective. Kids were not uncouth creatures who needed an education and a course in manners to be redeemed. No, there was something wondrous and unknowable about them. And if parents simply became a bit more passive around their kids at times, and opened their hearts and allowed their children's light to shine, they would connect to their children in a more authentic and less contrived manner.

In general, I grew up way too fast. I was not like Michael, who bypassed his childhood almost completely, but I missed many of its key components. First, there was my parents' divorce. Often, children of divorce cannot afford to remain kids. They face adult situations such as heartbreak and emotional trauma at an early age. They are frequently called upon to be caregivers to their parents, who are nursing painful wounds and a lot of guilt. And, if their parents are busy fighting custody and financial battles, such children are sometimes left, in the most literal way, to raise themselves.

The earliest indication I received that I was different from the boys who had remained, well, just regular boys was when I went to summer sleepover camp at age nine. Every night, the counselor would tell us all a bedtime story. He would then announce it was time for lights-out. He would bid us good night and exit the room, and soon everyone was fast asleep. Except me. I was dumbfounded. You mean these kids just put their heads on a pillow and fall asleep? You're kidding, right? That was never my experience. Every night, I would put my head on my pillow, toss and turn for two hours, think about all the things that troubled me, contemplate where G-d was, think about the broken shards of my soul, and eventually, when I couldn't keep my lids open any longer, fall asleep. And it was there at camp that I began to understand that the innocence of my childhood had eluded me.

As someone who grew up too fast, I did not always appreciate childlike qualities. For me, they were babyish. I didn't like doodling with crayons. I bought a moped at age twelve when the legal age was fifteen and drove all around Miami Beach. And finally, I left home to start rabbinical school and lived in a dormitory from age fourteen on. I was firmly in the camp of those who would look at someone like Michael Jackson, with his reading cartoons and climbing into his tree house, as a big baby.

But these conversations with Michael began to change my perspective. Maybe in my dismissal of my own childhood I had allowed myself to grow crusty and cynical. I prided myself on having started life early and accomplished certain goals in my twenties. But perhaps in the process I, too, had begun to see people as a means to an end. Perhaps the recognition of my hard work as rabbi at Oxford University and the even modest status that came from being a writer and broadcaster had become too important to me. How much of my innocence had I sacrificed?

And it was kind of overwhelming to watch, in our weekly and sometimes twice-weekly sessions, the leading entertainer of his generation get all excited about watching the Three Stooges on TV. Maybe Michael was right. Perhaps adult entertainment had become a little bit too violent, too exploitative, too corrupt.

To be sure, Michael took the immersion in a kids' world to an extreme. In the final analysis we all do grow up and we have to embrace adult responsibility, discover adult maturity, and live the life of a productive member of society. And Michael had to understand that his best friends simply could no longer be kids. They needed a peer group, just as he did.

But with some important modifications, Michael's vision begins to make real sense. What we should all seek to be is not Peter Pan, adult kids who never grow up. Rather, we should aim to be individuals who never forget the joys of being carefree and the wholesomeness of wearing our hearts on our sleeves. We have to be well-rounded adults on the outside. But this comes from never losing the child on the inside. This is the central concept that unfolds in the inspirational values Michael and I discuss in this book.

Michael once said to me in a haunting conversation, presented in *The Michael Jackson Tapes,* that if he were ever prevented from doing his work on behalf of children, he would choose death. To a large degree, Michael was prevented from working with children once people questioned his motives and serious allegations were made against him.

Michael wanted his life to become synonymous with a great cause. He wanted to make the world more innocent, more playful, more alive. And he hoped to achieve that by highlighting lessons from the world's children. Not being able to accomplish any of this slowly poisoned his soul. It caused him a level of pain so great that he destructively chose to escape it through the prescription drug addiction that ultimately consumed him.

But we who survive him can finally correct this injustice. Michael has engendered either fanatical loyalty or fanatical opposition. And somehow, in the midst of the squabble to address the mystery of Michael Jackson, the redemptive aspects of his message about children have been lost.

The truth of the matter is that there has seldom been a modern celebrity or world personality who put more mental and emotional energy into trying to understand the world of the child than Michael Jackson. And we can laugh it off if we wish. We can dismiss it as immature and regressive. But the amazing thing is that Michael would have welcomed the accusation of "childish" as a compliment. Had you accused him of being "adultish," he would have been insulted.

Michael once told me that he viewed adults as like dogs, and he wasn't saying it to be mean. When you buy an adult dog, he explained, you don't know what baggage it brings. Had it been abused by a previous owner? Had it become mean through neglect? And would it bite as a result? But a puppy has no history, and it could not hurt you. Michael felt that adults had hurt him. Much of his experience at the hands of adults was, he alleged, negative: parental aggression from a father he loved, the adoration of sycophants for his craft rather than his heart, and the false friendship of members of his entourage, feigned for personal gain. And though he did not say it, finally there were the doctors who pretended to be healers but allowed themselves to become his drug pushers instead. Children, by contrast, treated him like a normal person. To the tabloids he might have been "Whacko Jacko," and to his fans the "King of Pop." But to the kids he was just Michael. It was with them that he found the freedom that celebrity had stolen at age five.

⸺ ⸙ ⸺

Our world needs to rediscover its lost innocence. We need to believe that indeed one day, as Isaiah prophesied, nations will beat their swords into ploughshares. No man will again teach his son the art of war. Husbands and wives will find it in their hearts to love each other and not divorce, and parents and children will reach across a generational divide to create harmonious families. We all need to rediscover the hopefulness and purity of our youth. Michael, however imperfectly, was leading us back there. And even as we may choose not to follow him to that place completely, that doesn't mean we can't let him open our eyes just a wee bit wider.

Go ahead. Read on. Your lost childhood awaits.

Cherishing, Honor, and Respect

Thank you for making things so beautiful.

SB: You have a lot of awe and wonder in your life, don't you? Tell me what inspires you.

MJ: A beautiful sunset is awe-inspiring to me. I pray when I see something totally magnificent. I was praying the other day. These clouds came over the mountains and the sun was setting and it put a beautiful line in the sky with orange underneath. How could you not see that and go, "Wow." I said to myself, *G-d, the world is so beautiful. Look at the clouds. Thank you for making things so beautiful.* Clouds are important—you know they give us moisture, oxygen. They didn't have to be beautiful when you look up. They didn't have to be inspiring. It's that extra little touch.

SB: That's a childlike quality—that sense of awe and wonder that adults often lose because they become so functional. Don't you see that when you are around children? They are much more impressed by those awesome sights.

MJ: Yes. I don't see how anyone can lose that later on and take it for granted. I see G-d through my children. I speak to G-d through children. I thank Him every day for the blessing of my children. G-d's wonder is captured in a child.

SB: You've said many times that children are G-d's gift to us. What does that mean to you?

MJ: In my family we love children. If a baby or a child comes in, we all want to hug the child or pick him up. That's how my brothers and sisters are. I can't understand why people don't honor children, why they push them aside like they are nothing. That's what tomorrow becomes.

SB: Does that mean for you, if religions have holy objects, then the holiest object of all is a child? That children deserve reverence and honor and respect?

MJ: Yes, it does. Children need to be shown a little approval, that they are doing the right thing. To be kind and loving to someone who is giving, to sit on someone's lap. Children show that lovingness all the time. But they are afraid.

> *G-d's wonder is captured in a child.*

For example, when somebody gives a child something and they jump all over. The next time the person comes again, the child jumps all over them. Is it okay? Of course it is okay. Children need our smile of approval in a lot of ways and we don't give it. Shmuley, your children were just naturally appreciative of everything. It's sweet, all these letters and things. And as a parent, I know you do it, they win your approval, your smile of approval.

SB: So you feel these qualities are already in the child. All it takes for the parent to strengthen a child's loving qualities is to reinforce them by saying, "That's a good thing." You feel these qualities are already in the child and with simple acknowledgment the child then feels these are the qualities to develop—my kindness, my goodness, my appreciation, my gratitude.

MJ: Yes, I think adults and parents are too busy making them out to be who we want them to be instead of going with who they are inside and who they were brought to this planet to be. There are too many talented people who didn't win the approval of their parents for their talents and abilities and I think that is just terrible.

SB: Tell me about ambition, especially as it relates to children. You were ambitious and you still are. But is that a childlike quality? Because sometimes ambition can manifest itself as ruthlessness.

MJ: No. I think every child is born wanting to do a certain thing and wanting to be like somebody who reached a certain goal that they haven't. And adults make them feel as if, "Are you kidding? Come on. I want you to have a real job. What are your chances of making it, doing that?" The Wright brothers, who were bicycle makers, had a dream of wanting to take flight. People never talk about the abuses they went through, these two guys. Or Edison. Every invention, there was the world scoffing and feeding him negative information. Everyone. And he talked about it later. Disney, who was always told, "Don't be stupid." Come on, his own father told him that. "You want to draw? How about a real job?"

SB: So what do you want for Prince and Paris? Do you want them to tell you what their ambitions are?

MJ: Yeah. I already know. He tells me he wants to make movies. He sits and watches and calls out the shots.

SB: Wow. You find it easy to respect your children's dreams and ambitions. But Michael, it seems that too many people see children as a burden rather than as the pleasure they are. Kids are demanding. Parents today are pulled in every direction. And they can lose patience with their kids.

MJ: They completely see children as a burden. Yes, they do. I have seen how cruel people can be, how abusive, how judgmental, how they have hurt me. What has saved my life is children. This is true.

> *Always I try and be completely affectionate with my children. I look in their eyes every day and say, "I love you."*

SB: The pain that you live with dissolves when you're helping children? It makes you feel real joy and relieves the pain at your center.

MJ: Especially if I know kids are hurting, that hurts me the most. That hurts me more than anything. I can't pretend that I don't feel it because I feel it so strongly.

SB: You still have the hurt and pain of your childhood. Do you feel that you have now won your own parents' approval? Has your career vindicated you?

MJ: From my parents? Yes, they love what I do and I am just an extension of their alter ego or subconscious or whatever you want to call it. I think I fulfilled my father's dreams of what he himself wanted to become and he did it through his children. I really believe that.

SB: Did he ever say that to you?

MJ: No, he never said so directly. That would have been so nice.

SB: With all your success he never said, "My gosh, son, you made me proud."

MJ: Ohhh, I wish. But I can see that I won his love, his approval, because he would go, "Great show," like that. He is real tough. He is not, like, "You won me over." He is, like, "Great job."

SB: And your mother, does she say, "You made us so proud"?

MJ: Ahhh, yes, with hugs and kisses. She is very affectionate and emotional and outgoing and expressive of how she feels.

SB: I will give you an example. When Steven Spielberg made *Schindler's List* and his mother has a kosher restaurant . . .

MJ: I have been there. I sent her flowers there and everything.

SB: I was speaking to her as she came around to all the tables to say hello. I said, "You must be very proud of your son, because *Schindler's List* won the Oscar and educated the whole world about the Holocaust." She said, "Ah, there are no words to ever describe. . . ."

Do you feel that your parents said to you, "There is nothing you could have done to make us more proud of you"?

MJ: I think they feel that way. I really believe that.

SB: But you would like to have it verbalized more from your father.

MJ: Yes, that would mean a lot to me. He tries to say it, but I don't know if he can say it. He tries to get there, but it is difficult. It is difficult to be totally affectionate. That's why always I try and be completely affectionate with my children. I look in their eyes every day and say, "I love you," and they tell me all the time. They go, "My heart misses you." These are the words they use.

Childlike Innocence

Children are a reminder of…
what we have to remember.

SB: You're a father now, as well as a son. Has it changed your sense of childhood and innocence?

MJ: I'll tell you. I thought I was prepared to be a father, but I wasn't. All my life I've read about how wonderful children are. People would go, "What is up with you and babies?" I am always reading child psychology books. But it's so much more joyous than even that. Prince and Paris changed me in so many ways. I learn as much from them as they learn from me. You learn about having a good heart and being a good-spirited person. And the way I am, I try and imitate them. People always say, "Act your age." But I try and act more like children because they are the innocent, they are G-dlike, they are pure. I try to be as humble and sweet as they are.

SB: What you're saying is that rather than parents only focusing on molding and shaping their children to reflect their values, it is almost as if G-d gives us children so that we ourselves can become children again?

MJ: I really believe in that. Children are, like, a reminder of how we should stay, of what we have to remember. When the Apostles were arguing among themselves, "Who is the greatest in the eyes of Jesus?" and Jesus says, "Unless you behave like this child . . . humble yourself like this child. . . . [I assumed Michael was referring to the words of Jesus in Matthew 18: "At that time the disciples came to Jesus, saying, 'Who is the greatest in the kingdom of heaven?' And calling to him a child, he put him in the midst of them and said, 'Truly, I say to you, unless you turn and become like children, you will never enter the kingdom of heaven. Whoever humbles himself like this child is the greatest in the kingdom of heaven.'"] Which is true.

> *People always say, "Act your age."*
> *But I try and act more like children because they*
> *are the innocent, they are G-dlike, they are pure.*
> *I try to be as humble and sweet as they are.*

SB: But how have *you* retained your childlike qualities with all the pressures and expectations around you?

MJ: It's hard to even explain. I am just honest with myself. I don't think most people are honest with themselves. I let go and when I let go, it's that purest form of myself, the innocence.

SB: So you have thrown away the peer pressure, you are not going to become what people want you to be? But have you had to pay a price because of that?

MJ: Yes, a terrible price, but I'll never lose being childlike because it is where my heart is. It just never grew up with me, I don't know why. I don't want it to, but I think I have the heart of an innocent child and I am not patting myself on the back or anything. But I see life the way children see it. When they feel something, I feel it.

SB: So many of us lose that childlike innocence. We go from being big-hearted, big-minded, to being small-minded, petty-minded? How do we get trapped into believing innocence is bad until we squander our natural treasures, our natural childhood, and become what everyone wants us to be? One of your gifts, Michael, is that you saw early that adulthood has two sides. It can be mature and wise, but it also can be an empty suit, the embodiment of ruthless ambition and the wrong values, that the emperor had no clothes. You were able to say, "I don't want that. I want to stick with real joys, to dance like a kid, to be totally free."

MJ: The world forces us to grow up. It's all around us and it starts in kids, with the influence of other, bigger kids. When parents drop the kids off at school and kiss them good-bye, what does their child say? "Not now, Mom, my buddies are looking." Can't we show love to our own children? You know, because somewhere those other kids have been influenced by the world, like. They tease: "That's not cool . . . I have to be cool now." The message is instilled in their brain.

SB: The conformity and peer pressure work to extinguish their individual spark. You know, Abraham Lincoln said that all of us are born G-d's originals and we die man's copies.

MJ: That's great, that's exactly it, isn't it?

SB: There is a bright shining lie being told to our children. We are saying that when you're a kid you are in Eden. Adam and Eve were like kids. They embody all the childlike qualities. They have no airs, no artifice. And the serpent came to them and said, "This isn't life. This thing you call the Garden of Eden is immature. It's stupid. You should outgrow this childish nonsense real quick." The serpent comes and says to all the people, "Forget this childlike stuff." There's a whole world you are missing, and the people begin to believe that lie. They choose to leave Eden and follow the serpent out of that childlike state.

That's what is happening to our kids. It's not cool to be a kid. Kids are pushed to believe that "being adult"— being exposed to "adult" things—is better than being a kid. That it's better than innocence and the freedom of childhood. Then we wonder why their lives, when they get older, are built on such rickety foundations. They're like trees that have no roots.

MJ: If I had not been exposed to all kinds of adult things as a little kid, I would be doing them right now, because I would be feeling there was something that I am missing. Out of curiosity people want to see the world that they have never been exposed to. But I have seen it and done it.

But I'm the guy to say, "Look! Your life now is the most wonderful, magical experience. Don't try and force yourself to grow up. Don't try and force yourself to be like someone else. You have the rest of your life to be an adult. The magic is here. J. M. Barrie, who wrote *Peter Pan,* said it best. When his younger brother died at the age of twelve, he always felt envious because he said his brother never had to grow up. He'd be a boy forever and that's where the real gold is. That's what inspired *Peter Pan.* It's true. *Peter Pan* grew out of that. He felt his brother would be a boy forever, and he was.

SB: And you consider yourself Peter Pan insofar as you understand the need to always stay a child? But how do you relate to the character of Peter Pan? Just the fact that he didn't grow up, or that he was really hurt by the world?

MJ: Because he wanted to hold on to innocence forever and he knew what the golden magic of childhood was all about. He wanted us to all hold on to that and keep that forever. Because once you grow up, it's all gone and that's why Peter Pan is an ancient, ancient soul. He's like E.T. He has been around for millions and millions of years but he has never aged and he finds this family and he takes the children to Neverland where they stay young forever.

SB: Have you learned that secret of how to stay young?

MJ: In my heart, yes.

SB: After all the hatred that has been shown you, it hasn't corrupted you in any way? You have never felt bitter? People become cynical adults because sometimes the scars of the world sink in and the pain corrupts them internally. They can't afford to remain naïve or innocent. The world has taken advantage of their innocence. So they have to put their dukes up in order to protect themselves. How did you rise above that?

MJ: For me, I rise above that because I believe in the truth. I believe in children—in becoming childlike again. If we can teach everybody to believe in children, that, I think, is the secret. I really do.

> *[Nature] is like soul food for us. We need it.*
> *That's what I think nature is. We need it.*

SB: But the average person, if they were shown a lot of hatred, they would either hate back or they would be less trusting, at least.

MJ: It is not in me to be like that. I try to be loving, and I try to find love and see love in all things. I love nature, I love the forest. I love the grace, the gentleness, the easiness of how gentle nature is. It is just giving. I love that.

SB: Do you see nature as the child's world and the city as the adult's world?

MJ: Yes. I am not street-smart at all. I hate the city. I love nature.

SB: The city is all about tall buildings and imposing struc-
ture. For you, nature is subtle and gentle, and warm and
embracing?

MJ: Yes, and giving. I love it. Children and nature go together.

SB: When you built Neverland, was it your special place to
protect yourself, the way Adam and Eve being in the
Garden of Eden was about them inhabiting a natural
paradise? It's a place where you could retreat and be
nourished?

MJ: Yes. I could walk around and know that I am not being
spied at and become one with nature and climb a tree and
do a load of stuff that I never got to do as a child. And I
love it. When I am up in that tree and I can be surrounded
by this world of branches and leaves and I can hear the
trickle of the water below and I am in heaven. I am in the
perfect paradise and I feel I could do anything. That's
what I am like when I am around children. I could do
anything. There is no limit to what I can do.

SB: And if you brought the adults of the world into Neverland, do you think that would be like a baptism of sorts?

MJ: Absolutely. I don't see how that cannot change a person.
We are drawn by water. There is something about our
souls that needs water. We flock to beaches, even if we
don't swim. We park our car there just to look out on the
calming of the ocean. It's like therapy, it's like meditation.
It's like soul food for us. We need it. That's what I think
nature is. We need it. Some of the great creative people

throughout history, when they were stuck or frustrated or worked too hard, and they would go to the forest or take these long outdoor adventures and then come back re-freshed. We need that. That's what vacation is all about.

SB: You know in the Bible in the Garden of Eden it says there were four rivers flowing through—water was a central part of it. You are very in touch with that story without even knowing it. Call it Peter Pan, call it what you will. It is an attempt to re-create Paradise, because children live in that sense of Paradise.

MJ: What makes me happiest is when I see a bunch of kids having fun in a beautiful environment where there is water, trees. I like lakes for the still water (I am a little in-timidated by the ocean), and they are all playing and there is grass and rolling hills and trees. There is nothing more magical than that. Remember that scene in *The Sound of Music* where they are in the Alps and the kids are tossing the ball back and forth and Julie Andrews has the guitar? The camera pulls back and you see these monumental mountains. Man. And the sunlight is in the right place and they have got the silver lining around their hair and it is a wide-angled lens. It is just a beautiful moment.

SB: Have you ever been there, by the way? Obersalzberg, in Austria?

MJ: Yes. I loved it. We have driven through there in winter. I love that part of the world. I have to have it. That's what I like about Roosevelt because he conserved and preserved a lot of the national parks. Yosemite would have been destroyed by now. It would have been high-rises with people ruining it.

SB: You want to empower people to hold on to their child nature and childlike spirit, don't you? It seems that adults start out really big and get smaller. They get diminished through all the pain and trials of life. They start sweet, sweet as kids, but they begin to sour. When a fruit gets detached from a tree, in the first few days it's okay, but then it begins to wither. Kids are so much closer to that natural source, aren't they, and they're therefore sweeter. But how do we teach adults to reconnect so that they don't decay—so they don't become more materialistic, bitter, and forlorn? Not some sort of fictional fountain of youth but some source of nature and paradise they can find *on the inside.* The Fountain of Youth is always there. And you believe that you've tapped into it. So you need to lead people to its source. We have to identify how adults lose that G-dly nature as they grow older and become more materialistic and more forlorn. What happens to them? Do you see that in your industry?

MJ: With celebrities, they try to be the way they expect the world to see them. "It's time for me to act eighteen, grow up. Let's go, baby, and pick up all the girls. Let's go dancing, let's boogie on down." They think that whatever is on that big screen is what they are supposed to have become at that stage. But that is someone else's theory and concept of living and life. That doesn't mean you should follow it. They are forgetting the magic is over here.

SB: So I want to ask you what Neverland means to you. You put your mind and your money and your heart into this place. Was it some sort of Eden, some sort of Paradise, you were trying to create?

MJ: To tell you the truth, I was just creating the world the way I would like to see it and creating in my life things I never got to do as a child, like rides and movie theaters. So I wanted everything I wanted to do behind my gates because I know I can't go out into the world and I wanted it to be a place to bring sick kids who are deprived and underprivileged from around the world, a haven for them where they can feel safe and have some escapism. Or kids who never got to see this type of thing in the inner cities, to breathe fresh air and see the mountains and all of that. I see Neverland being a lot more water. I want lots more cascades and caves and it needs a lot more water. That's how I see it. I think water is healing and animals are the greatest therapy . . . nature.

SB: But is it to take kids out of reality and put them in this place? Or is it so that kids can be immersed in that place and it can spread? Do you want to make the rest of the world like that? Is Neverland a model or a haven?

MJ: I think it's the perfect hypothesis because I think people, when they come, they feel so much better afterwards. They feel rejuvenated, they feel healed . . . and I have seen it. It transforms people. It is nature and it is love. But it is the music that gets into the grass and makes the trees grow more beautifully and the birds come around. I keep that synergy going all the time. When you get children there you can touch it, you can feel the innocence. The deer come and I love all of that. That's the world I live in.

SB: So it *is* like a Garden of Eden—music, beauty, animals, no one being harmed—to have all of the world's delight at your fingertips.

Creativity and Inspiration

All [of the] most creative people
act just like children.

SB: When Prince and Paris were born, did it change how you looked at your career, your music, your creativity, everything?

MJ: They get great priority in my life. The work that I do now, it is almost as if it has to be the highest form of my creative ability because they inspire that in me . . . they inspire me.

SB: So, while they are the priority of your life, you are also saying that they have enhanced your career because you are more artistic, you have more inspiration in your life. The first thing I ever said to you on the phone when I called you was, "Hi, Michael, is that your son in the background?" You said, "Yes, that's my son. They're the best. Aren't they the best?" That's the first thing you said to me.

Is that a part of your creativity, that you can be natural around Prince and Paris and other children and you can't be natural around adults? You're not a superstar to the kids. You are just Michael.

MJ: They don't care and I can be myself and jump into their magical world. That's the world I have always lived in all my life. That's the level and the consciousness that all great creativity comes from, all genius, be it the sculptor, the artist, a painter, that level of childlike innocence. It comes from that line. It really does. It's that purity of G-d, and I think we haven't scratched the surface of understanding who children are.

Children become conditioned by the system and what people call "peer pressure" and trying to adjust to the way we think we ought to be—act your age, be a teenager, I wanna be a man—and they lose that golden magical thing that is becoming not child*ish*, but childlike. All creativity, from Michelangelo's work to Spielberg to George Lucas . . . all [of the] most creative people act just like

> *All great creativity comes from, all genius, be it the sculptor, the artist, a painter, that level of childlike innocence.*

children. They will be playing little games like Nintendo or reading comic books, and most people would be shocked to know this. But I am around these people and I see it and I know it. I do it. I have comics and I love it. Our children are the most golden thing we have and to see what's happening, for me to see the problems we are having in the world with our children, and I think I pretty much understand why. This is the greatest one-word message of all time, it's *love*. And children teach you how to love.

SB: In Oxford, all the greatest minds, many are like kids. They're famously eccentric. Their shirts are always out.

Their hair is never brushed. They don't know where they are half the time. They are always losing things. They are the quintessential absent-minded professors. Look at Robin Williams and how "immature" he can be. I don't mean that in a derogatory way.

MJ: I love when he acts like that. And Jim Carrey when he acts nutty. I love that.

SB: John Belushi, I think, used to say his creativity used to come from cocaine. But it's the same kind of thing, be-

> *I've heard that the cells in the body actually move to the rhythm of the music we're listening to. . . . And children are physically moved by rhythm. They feel it in their body.*

cause for him cocaine set him free because he was too limited, too rigid. It was his way of transcending limitation and inhibition, albeit in the most destructive possible way. It's the same as getting drunk. People take alcohol in order to loosen their inhibitions. There are just different ways of inner liberation and freedom. There is the negative, damaging, deadly way to do so, like drugs and alcohol, or there is a healthy way and that is to return to innocence.

Picasso once said that every child is born an artist, which we, of course, see since they love to draw. Do you think children are also innately musical?

MJ: I've heard that the cells in the body actually move to the rhythm of the music we're listening to. And they've been shown to respond differently to oboe or flute or bassoon. And children are physically moved by rhythm. They feel it in their body.

SB: Children's reaction to music seems so intuitive. It comes naturally. And you seem to have retained that natural movement. You just have to move.

MJ: I have to. I can't help it. I'll hear music playing and wonder why nobody else is moving. My body just has to. A real dancer is a person who can interpret the sounds he hears. You become the bass, you become the drum, you become the violin, the oboe. And this is all internal, not external. It's not about thinking. That's why when a dancer starts to count—one and two and three—he's thinking and all that should be gone. You can see it on their face if they're counting. Your expression has to be in line with what you're feeling in your body. So, in what I do, I don't even know where I'm going. It's just improvisation. It creates itself. But you still have to put your body through hell to express yourself. You have to be that dedicated.

Curiosity

[Children] are fascinated by everything.

SB: You've said that people who are still creative and imaginative are all childlike. Talk to me about your curiosity. How does it express itself? Does it manifest itself in a pursuit of knowledge? I know you have an extensive library of books, many of them leather-bound special editions.

MJ: I am just curious about all things, the simplest things. About what is in a drop of water. I wanted to read about eyelashes one time and found out a whole colony of living things live in our eyelashes. To me that's amazing. Everything to me is interesting, especially if you start studying the universe and all that. It is just a phenomenal amount of information and I am just astounded by it. It makes me feel ignorant about how much I don't know. The more I find out, the more ignorant I feel. I really do. I realize there is so much to learn. That's why bookstores amaze me. I can spend hours and hours grabbing books and I come back with boxes of stuff. That's one of the things I love about my mother. We used to go to the bookstore and spend hours and she let us get whatever we wanted. She let us have it, she never said no. We would read, read, read. I love that. It is just wonderful, isn't it? I am very curious about everything. There is nothing I am not interested in.

SB: You retained the wonderful curiosity of a child?

MJ: Yes. I pick up things and people go, "What are you looking at that for?" And there will be a leaf on the ground and I will pick it up and study it. I am fascinated by it. Or you look at a bug real hard and you start thinking about everything, like how tiny its heart and the brain are and whether they think the way we do. I want to know all those things. I wish I could understand more things. I wish I had time to research and learn and know and ask, because I am so curious about the universe. It amazes me about certain things and animals and you find out stuff like how a sea-

> *Everything to me is interesting, especially if you start studying the universe. . . . The more I find out, the more ignorant I feel. . . . That's what I love about children. . . . They are curious.*

horse gives birth to a baby, the male gives birth. Or how certain South American frogs can change sexes, like if he's a man, he changes into a woman. I find that, like, odd and weird and unbelievable. I love stuff like that.

SB: Do you think adults are as curious, or do they lose a lot of their curiosity?

MJ: A lot of them lose it. I can't watch things without asking, "Why does that happen?" Did you ever see birds that migrate, hundreds of them at the same time? How do they know to do their choreography at the same time? What is it? Is it telepathy? Why don't we do it as humans? That amazes me.

SB: So how did you retain your curiosity? A lot of people make a lot of money, become famous, and they are not as curious because they don't have to look as hard anymore. They just become curious about how to buy a bigger airplane.

MJ: I think some people are more curious than others. I think as children we all have the same level of it. I really believe that. But some people just lose it on the way. That's what I love about children. They are fascinated by everything. That's why you see them breaking a lot of things, tearing them up, because they want to know how it works and the only way they know is to break it. They don't realize; they are taking it apart to study and we go, "No, don't do that, don't touch." We should let them. They are curious. They want to see what is inside.

SB: In raising Prince and Paris, do you always try to encourage their curiosity?

MJ: Absolutely. I made Prince stop watching television today on the way here to look out of the window. And he looked out of the window and started naming everything. "What are they carrying in that truck?" "I think they are carrying fruits and vegetables." "Why?" "Because they are probably taking it to the market. Somebody has picked it . . ." He was coming up with all these great questions about everything outside the window and I felt this was great. He had a lot of good questions. But he does some things which are really scary to me. He sits and watches the television and calls out every shot that the cameraman is doing and that the director decides to do. So he sits there going, "The camera is moving up for a close-up. Now it is moving back. Now it's going . . ." He is naming every shot. I didn't teach him to do this. He sits there and says it out loud. He is literally putting the movie together. I think that is amazing. I don't know how he learned that, because he is interested in cameras and film.

I bought him his own camera and he makes his own movies and he directs Paris. He says, "You stand here and I want you to walk over here." I have footage of him directing. I think it is really sweet. I love it. My mother said I did that when I was little, that I was choreographing and giving all the brothers their notes and telling them how to move. She would say she would watch me and be amazed not knowing where I got it from, but I would do all the choreography, all the harmonies, and she said she was just astounded not knowing that I knew all this. When people ask me where does it come from, I go, "Er, it comes from above and it just works through me." I can't create it. It has to be a channel. It really does.

SB: So this childlike curiosity that you've retained, you didn't really work on it. You just believe it is a divine gift. Do you feel grateful to G-d for it?

MJ: It is a divine gift, Shmuley, it is. When the gift of song and the gift of dance come into my head and pop into my lap, like a lady giving birth, I literally get on my knees and I say thank you.

Forgiveness, Friendship, and Loyalty

*Children fight, but they forgive
each other in a second.*

SB: Children fight, but they forgive each other in a second. A moment later they're playing together again. Adults harbor grudges. Do you learn forgiveness from children?

MJ: Children become friends in a second and they forgive in a second. It's the grown-ups who teach them how to hold a grudge. "Oh no, you are not playing with her, re-

> *Sometimes we are taught by adults to hold a grudge and be moody and vindictive, to hate, to become racist and prejudiced, all the evils of mankind.... That's taught, that's conditioning, that doesn't come naturally.*

member what she did the other day. I am not going to let you forget this." They are ready to forgive in a second and I am like that. Sometimes we are taught by adults to hold a grudge and be moody and vindictive, to hate, to become racist and prejudiced, all the evils of mankind, that is embedded in the hearts of . . . the places where people go and they become ugly and vindictive. That's taught, that's conditioning, that doesn't come naturally. I think kids will start to fight the way that puppies start to bite one another but it turns into play. They'll forgive so fast. To hold a grudge and just become hateful, I think that's taught.

SB: We see that children aren't like that, so something along the way changes them. Have they taught you forgiveness? Have you had an experience in life . . . well, you have told me that people have looked you in the eye and cried and a year later they have sued you. Naturally it is hard to be forgiving after a while. Have children taught you to be more forgiving?

MJ: Children have taught me to be always forgiving. People, like I said, become hateful and vindictive because of conditioning. Someone whispers in their ear, "This guy is loaded. We are going to make this happen. We are going to get a piece of this," like that. That kind of thing is where people get into trouble. It's like the serpent whispering in the ear, saying, "No, no, no, no, we are going to do this." But that's when G-d should come in, that side of the person, and say, "No, that's not the right thing to do. We are going to do this and this." It's sad that people can't be more like children. I don't mean childish, but childlike.

SB: They say that a dog is man's best friend, dogs are loyal.

MJ: I totally disagree with that. It has got a lot of people into trouble, that expression.

SB: What people mean is that these dogs are always loyal. Are children loyal?

MJ: Children, I think, can be very loyal. I hate to say it, but it's according to how you shape and mold them. But I think nothing is more trusting than a good child. I see children as dolphins for a lot of reasons. I think dolphins should get the credit for being man's best friend when it comes to animals, not dogs. They are always good.

SB: So dogs can be mean?

MJ: Very, they can turn on you. I have seen it. I have seen our dogs turning on me after being completely good to them.

SB: You believe in loyalty, I know.

MJ: You have to be loyal. That is so important, after what I have been through.

SB: That's what I mean. How do you believe in loyalty when you have seen how many people haven't been?

MJ: A lot of adults, they sell out to what they think people want to hear. A parent can mold them into doing that and believing that. A good child will not do that. You show them a good time and the next day they are all over you with love and hugs and kisses, unless the parent says, "Wait a minute, you watch him. What he did is not normal." They make the child think some people are weird or strange when there is nothing weird or strange about them. You hear it in their voice the next day, completely out of jealousy. I have seen it happen.

Giving and Generosity

I always had this yearning to give and help.

SB: You know the ancient rabbis said that every time you visit someone sick, you take away one-sixtieth of their illness. But with you, it's almost like you take away 50 percent of their illness. [I had just brought a mentally challenged young man to meet Michael, and he lit up at meeting his singing idol.]

MJ: Yeah, yeah. I don't like to see anybody hurt or suffer, especially children.

SB: Do you feel that you have a healing power that was given to you? Or is it because of the celebrity? In other words, being a great celebrity, when you show a child attention, they feel really good. They know how famous you are, they feel like, "Wow, someone that famous cares about me, I must be special." But is it beyond celebrity? Is it something in you that you had before celebrity?

MJ: I think it's something that I'm supposed to do because I always had this yearning to give and help and make people feel better in that way.

SB: You had this before, when you were Michael Jackson the boy?

MJ: Yes. If there is someone who isn't feeling well or sick, making them feel happy, feel better, especially if you can turn them around and help save them. I love doing that. I love going to hospitals to see the children. What I don't like is when all the grown-ups and the doctors and the nurses take pictures and all the attention. They are much worse than the kids. They take all the attention away from the kids. They turn it into a zoo. They do. I love holding babies.

SB: I told you that story about Stephen Hawking, the great Cambridge physicist, about how much he loves holding babies. When he was my guest as a speaker at Oxford. My wife had just given birth to our sixth child and Hawking insisted on holding the baby. His wife, who told me that her husband loves babies, took his lifeless arms and gently

> *I always had this yearning to give and help and make people feel better in that way.*

wrapped them around the infant in an incredible display of affection.

MJ: I love babies.

SB: All these things bring you joy?

MJ: Absolutely.

SB: Tell me about your relationship with Mother Teresa.

MJ: She used to write to me a lot, long letters, and ask me to come to Calcutta to do a show, but you can't. It's hard to explain to her why it couldn't be done. She'd say how I was a gift from G-d, an angel, thank me for the work I did for children and how the children here love you. "Please try to find a way to come here and do a show." And she was very serious. Because of the scale of Diana's popularity, Diana overshadowed Mother Teresa, but she actually did much more work than Diana, over a much wider span. Diana's heart was in the right place, but when Mother Teresa died, it wasn't as big as it should have been. [Diana died a day before Mother Teresa, and the death of the princess completely overshadowed that of the living saint.] An international treasure was lost, but people wanted to talk more about Diana.

> *Entertainment is about taking people away from the regular order of things when there is some chaos and pain and stress.*

SB: So even Mother Teresa saw great value in entertainment and how it could uplift these special kids?

MJ: Entertainment is about taking people away from the regular order of things when there is some chaos and pain and stress. You become entertained or charmed by something, be it a show . . . that's important. We all need an escape if we can get it.

SB: Do you think your children, Prince and Paris, are going to understand that you are a loving father who did everything for them, to the best of your ability, even if you paid so much attention to other children?

MJ: If they ever start saying, "What about us? You were always running off to help this child or that child," I'll take them with me and then they can see why. "You want me to ignore this, and turn my head as if I don't see it? Would you like to help this child live?" And they'll say, "Yes." Then they'll understand. We are going to take toys to hospitals and orphanages and stuff like that. I like the way Lady Diana would make her kids wait in line. There are pictures of them in the lines. That impressed me so much. Prince Harry and William in line like everyone else. That was good.

SB: Did you feel an immediate connection with her?

MJ: Yes, I loved her very much, always.

SB: Did she show you a lot of love?

MJ: We confided in each other, privately. I miss her too much. Too much, yes. Too much.

Gratitude and Thankfulness

I can't take credit for everything I do. . . .
There is always some higher source.

SB: You don't want to spoil your children, you don't want them to ever take things for granted. You make sure that they are not spoiled. Even though there is candy everywhere in Neverland, they can have it, you told me, only on their birthdays or maybe on days when special guests come. You want Prince and Paris to appreciate their blessings.

MJ: Well, when somebody gives them something, I want them to really appreciate it and not to ever be arrogant. When they get the smallest little thing they go nuts. People go, "Wow," because it is a little thing and people are impressed by how they are not spoiled because they think they get everything. But I don't let them get overtaken by it. There is so much stuff in storage and we put it away.

SB: So children have the capacity to be spoiled and you have to prevent it. Like Grace [the children's nanny], when we were with the kids at Neverland, she said she wouldn't let them go on the big rides, she said, "I want Prince and Paris to appreciate this."

MJ: They don't get to go on the rides much at all. Only on special occasions, like if your family comes over or a certain family in the area. I don't ever want them to feel like it doesn't impress them. That would be so disappointing.

SB: You always want them to share. You don't want them to be possessive about Neverland and about the toys. Even when we have bought them presents and you say, "Oh, say 'Thank you.'" Manners are very important to you, how they behave.

MJ: Yes, it is a reflection of the adults. It is important.

SB: You also don't want them to be possessive about Neverland and about the toys.

MJ: Never like, "This is mine and this is not yours." Urggh. I never want them to be like that. That would be so embarrassing. It is very important to share. We share our house. We let the public in. We let the children in from all walks of life, from all nations. They have to know that. We don't discriminate in any way.

SB: You've often said you wished you had moments of celebration with your family, Sabbath dinners and such.

MJ: Oh G-d, yeah. People have to come together.

SB: Like what birthdays are about. This is a very interesting point. You're saying that the whole purpose of these holidays is mostly as a meeting ground, as a rendezvous point, a context for people to join together.

MJ: That's right, that's right.

SB: It seems that showing gratitude to the people who gave to you as a child and even today is very important to you. Specifically, Berry Gordy, who discovered you at Motown, you have always tried to show—even after you got the label and you could have forgotten about him—you always tried to show him recognition and got him into concerts and always acknowledged him publicly. So speak to me about gratitude.

MJ: Yes, very much. To be gracious and have gratitude and show appreciation for those who have been good to you and who have lifted you up in times of need, who have been a great aid to your life. I have always appreciated those who have helped me down the road when I so much

> *To be gracious and have gratitude and show appreciation for those who have been good to you and who have lifted you up in times of need, who have been a great aid to your life. I have always appreciated those who have helped me down the road when I so much needed it so many times in my life.*

needed it so many times in my life. I don't see how I could have forgotten the kindnesses done to me.

SB: Then there are a lot of people who you really gave them their break, like Wesley Snipes, whom you launched in a music video. Or even Elton John. I read he was one of your opening acts in Liverpool or somewhere.

MJ: Yeah, before he became famous he opened up for the queen of England, several things like that.

SB: Do you think people have responded with the same kind of gratitude?

MJ: To me, showing thanks? Not the way they should have. Some do, some don't. I think maybe in the future they will see, I hope. But you know, whatever.

SB: Do you feel hurt when people don't show you that kind of gratitude? I know I find it hurtful if I help someone with something and later they just forget you and they become very self-absorbed.

MJ: Yeah, it can be hurtful.

SB: In terms of instilling a sense of gratitude in your children, you want them to be grateful for the little things, the big things?

MJ: That is very important. That's right. And everything I do and other people do, to be thankful for the smallest little things, to say, "Thank you" and "You're welcome."

SB: But usually when someone becomes very famous and very successful, they do forget the people on the bottom of the ladder.

MJ: I don't understand that.

SB: Why do you remember them? How do you remember them?

MJ: Because I am sensitive to other people's feelings and emotions . . . and I am very thankful. I don't know if I could have done what I have done without the help of other people on the way, really. Even those who don't know how much they helped me, I thanked them later. Even those who do things from a distance and don't know that it is affecting me from another place. Like writers and entertainers, people who died before when I was just a toddler.

SB: Did you ever call anyone up and say, "Hi, I'm Michael Jackson. I just wanted to say thank you because, you don't even know this, but you made a difference."

MJ: Yes. From Sammy [Davis, Jr.] to James Brown to Jackie Wilson to Walt Disney, who I pray for all the time. I try to seek out their families if they have a wife left, a widow. Charlie Chaplin. I go to his grave and I pray. I never met Charlie. I go and get on my knees and I pray. We [Michael looked at his children] love Charlie Chaplin. I don't know if I could be the same entertainer without Charlie Chaplin and Jackie Wilson and Sammy Davis, Jr. I wouldn't. They taught me a lot. About timing and rhythm and pathos and all those great things.

SB: Also, I read that you went to visit Charlie Chaplin's widow?

MJ: Yes, I did. I was in my glory.

SB: Was that out of gratitude?

MJ: Yes. I had to say thank you to someone that was close to him. I said, "You don't understand." Or like what happened with Shirley Temple and I said, "Thank you." She said, "For what?" I said, "For everything you have done. You have saved my life," and she didn't understand. I explained to her. Like the times when I felt I couldn't make it anymore, just having her presence there did it for me.

SB: Relating that to a childlike experience, do you think that gratitude is something that children naturally feel? You give them something and they appreciate it, they feel close to you if you give them a little present. If you play with them, they don't forget you the way adults sometimes forget?

MJ: I think that is normal with children. Parents teach them to do the opposite, to be, like, "Don't talk to him," to be cold and mean. But there are some good people. So I think they should teach children how to be loving and to

> *[Parents] should teach children how to be loving and to understand goodness and real genuine quintessential kindness.*

understand goodness and real genuine quintessential kindness. That's important.

SB: Part of that has to do with humility. You are not afraid to admit that who you are today, a lot of people contributed to that. Maybe other people want to be arrogant about it and say, "I am responsible for my own success. I worked hard."

MJ: I never say that. I am responsible for a lot of my circumstances, but there are a lot of people who have been there for me who have helped me along the way. I can't take credit for everything I do. I don't know if I can take credit for anything I do. There is always some higher source, just like a channel.

SB: G-d is the highest. So you are always thankful to Him and that is part of your gratitude?

MJ: Are you kidding? Of course.

SB: What would you say is the greatest gift G-d gave to you?

MJ: The gift of curiosity, life, love.

SB: Now that you've become a parent, does it make you understand your own parents more?

MJ: G-d, I don't know how my mother did it. I have two, she had ten. I don't know how she did it.

SB: Does that make you love her and appreciate her more?

MJ: Yeah, I cry more now. She was handicapped, she had polio and I . . . I don't know how she did that. I really don't.

SB: Do you feel a real sense of gratitude to her?

MJ: Yeah, she thanks me, Shmuley. She's always thanking me. She always says, "Thank you for everything you've done for me." And I go, "Mother, what are you talking about?" "Look what you've done for me," I said. "Don't thank me. Thank you."

Hope and
the Divine

*[Children] are G-d's way of saying there is
hope, there is such a thing as humanity.*

SB: The Bible says that men and women are all created in G-d's image, they are all G-d's children. But that, you are saying, is belief. I look at men and women and have to believe that they possess a spark of the divine. It's a matter of faith. But with children there is no faith. You see it. So as we get older that visibility that we are part of G-d is somehow lost. By loving children you are able to love G-d.

MJ: By loving children I am able to see G-d. I see G-d through children. If it wasn't for children I would not understand what G-d is, who He is, no matter what the Bible says, even though I love the Bible. But children are proof. You can write and talk all you want, but I see it. Man, do I see it.

Children—this is my opinion—represent the purest, the quintessence of honesty, of love, of G-d. To me they are G-d's way of saying there is hope, there is such a thing as humanity. Be like children, be humble like them, be sweet, be giving, be innocent. It shows in the eyes, I always see it in eyes. When you look in a child's eyes you see just a pure innocence and it reminds me to be humble, to be sweet, and to be really good. I don't mean to sound weird, but I really believe that children are G-d. I think they are the purest form of the creation of G-d. When a child steps in the room I am totally changed. I feel their energy, their presence, and their spirit. I think we have to remember it is so easy for adults and parents to push them aside and not to pay attention to them. But I think they have so much to say and we don't listen, we don't feel. It's almost hard to put it into words.

SB: What happens when they grow older? Do they lose those special qualities as they become adults, or do they retain them? And do you, personally, feel you are more in touch with those special qualities when you are around them?

> *If we can hold on to the magic, to that child that lives inside of you and me, that is still there, I think that's the greatest magic in the world.*

MJ: I think society and, of course, just being in the world, and learning what we think is the way to be, the way to do . . . stereotyping, whatever. It's what changes people and through things like the media and television and movies and radio we learn and we see what we should do and should become. But I think if we can hold on to the magic, to that child that lives inside of you and me, that is still there, I think that's the greatest magic in the world. I really do. I really, really do. There is nothing like that to me and I play off of that. Everything I created and all of my art and all of my talent that was given to me is completely inspired by children—nothing more than that. Every song I have written, from "Billie Jean" to "Beat It" to "Heal the World" to "We Are the World," that's from children.

And when I feel like I am in a bind, which happens creatively sometimes, I have a couple of kids over or be around children, and I feel like I am unbounded. I can do anything. There is really no limit to my creativity and it is completely inspired by them and G-d. It's the same thing.

SB: You see them as really a part, a spark of G-d here on earth?

> *There is nothing more pure and spiritual to me*
> *than children and I cannot live without them.*
> *If you told me right now, "Michael, you can never see*
> *another child," I would kill myself.*

MJ: I swear they are. There is nothing more pure and spiritual to me than children and I cannot live without them. If you told me right now, "Michael, you can never see another child," I would kill myself. I swear to you I would because I have nothing else to live for. That's it. Honestly. Children have saved me every second of my life. My mother knows this. I would throw in the towel in a second but they [children] are making me hold on, because they show me love and it's like G-d saying, "Everything is going to be okay." It's like when there are dark clouds all over the sky and you see that little patch of blue and it's like G-d saying, "Everything is going to be fine."

SB: If you are really down or something is really bothering you and you see a child, it's like G-d saying, "Take it easy."

MJ: That's exactly as it is, Shmuley. You said it. And every time I have felt at the end of my rope, some kind of kid would show up somewhere. Just when I can't take it anymore and I really want to just die, I really do. Boom! It hits me, and I get on my knees and I thank G-d. I do, Shmuley. That's why I believe in it. I really do. Elizabeth [Taylor] knows it. She says, "The way you love babies and children is the way I love diamonds."

SB: It's a great line. But you see them being more precious than diamonds?

MJ: Much more precious than diamonds. A diamond doesn't give me joy. It's sparkly and it's pretty, yes. It's a material thing. I can't talk to a diamond. I can't show emotion to a diamond. Children are the entire world.

SB: If you go to Auschwitz . . .

MJ: I've been there. When I was little.

SB: They take you through the whole museum and it's devastating and at the end there is a panel showing two little girls skipping rope. The idea is that after all the devastation and horrors of the Holocaust, there are still kids playing in playgrounds today. There is still a sun shining. There is still hope. No matter how bad you think it is, a kid is still playing, right?

MJ: Yes.

SB: And that means it is going to be okay.

MJ: They are going to find some amazing things about children not only this century, this decade, they really are. Stuff that was there all along, amazing things about the mind of children and how incredibly amazing they are. G-dlike. I really believe that. People are going to open the door to a lot of brilliance . . . the outlook on children is going to change. I have never talked down to Prince and Paris. I never do because they are amazing. You can't, they are *much* smarter than we think. The baby-talk thing is going to go away. You won't do the "goo goo ga ga." They are so smart, they understand as intellectuals everything we say. They are much brighter than anyone could ever imagine. They are in alpha state. They understand the subconscious. We don't understand. We are the ones that really don't understand who they are.

SB: They are born with some kind of knowledge?

MJ: A lot of knowledge. I think they know a lot that we haven't come yet to understand. They *are* the universe. They really are. Most people don't get it.

SB: Do you think you were born with a special sensitivity to children?

MJ: I can't say how I was when I was a toddler, but my mother always told me that children always came knocking on the door asking, could they see Michael? Could they play with me? This is when I was really little. No fame, just a little bitty kid of two or three. I didn't work at it. I just care about other people putting children aside all the time. They don't care about them and they say, "Sit down and shut up." I know what they are feeling. I understand their feelings. G-d forbid, when they are sick it's even worse. They are the sunshine of the world. It's hard to put it into words . . . it is so special to me.

SB: It's like an infinite G-dly presence that can't be explained. There are no obstructions in children. So Divine energy flows through.

> *I think G-d talks to us through children. I really do.*

MJ: I think G-d talks to us through children. I really do.

SB: Do you know the ancient rabbis said that? In the Talmud, they said that 2,000 years ago . . . they said that prophecy is expressed through children.

MJ: Did they really? It's true. I see it so much.

SB: So you are never bored of children?

MJ: No. I am never bored with them. I may get bored at the end of the day or something, but no, no way.

SB: Has that helped the development of Prince and Paris, that you are able to talk to them as equals?

MJ: If you talk down, you are creating that level that they are talking on. You talk on a higher level, they will accept it on that level. Whatever level you choose they will accept it on, and that's the truth. You can communicate with them on that very level. You created the standard because they are an open slate and they are so brilliant. They are, like, saying to you, "Whatever you want, I'll get it," because they are so bright and fast. It's true.

Humor, Play, and Laughter

Just let go and be free-spirited.

SB: To what extent is humor important in your life? You are always joking, throwing little things with [your close friend] Frank [Cascio], doing silly things, laughing out loud. How important is humor to children? How important is humor for adults in their quest to become more childlike?

MJ: I think personally it is one of the most important qualities to have because you can play and just let go and be free-spirited. And that's part of being childlike. Some people may look at it as though you are being an imbecile. "Behave yourself!" But it's fun. You gotta play. I love that.

SB: Has humor taken off a lot of the pressures that you are subjected to? If you have a big concert coming up, you can fool around with members of the band or with people you are close to, like Frank?

MJ: You know the best thing for me before a concert is I have a couple of children come backstage and I meet them and shake their hands. I give them a hug. When we do "Heal the World," the children come out and they are all dressed in their cultural native costumes and they all hold hands around a giant globe. So to make them feel comfortable with me, I meet them before the show so that they can kinda know me a little bit, so when they are onstage they are not staring me in the face going, "Oh my G-d, it's Michael Jackson." Just that feeling of them back there with me, I feel like I am ready to go out and conquer the world. It is all the fuel and energy I need to make that concert rock. The crowds are stomping like this. They want the show to start. It is a great energy. You have to feel that backstage sometime. Peek behind and see the sea of faces, over 100,000 people, and they are chanting and they are doing the wave and you go, "Oh my G-d, oh my G-d. I love it. *Love it!*"

We are going to find out in this next century that there is something really magical about laughter.... I think some kind of chemical reaction takes place in the soul.

SB: Why do you feel more comfortable in bigger crowds than small crowds?

MJ: That is where I was born. I was born onstage entertaining. That's my element. To be amongst crowds and people and entertain. That's when I am comfortable. When you bring it down in scale, I get a bit shy. I get a bit, "Ooh, you are staring at me." I can't take it. I get a bit uncomfortable.

SB: Is it the fact that you are making an impact on them, on large audiences, but in crowds they are looking at you and you're thinking, "What do they want?"

MJ: When I am entertaining I am . . . I am in control. I take them where I want to take them and I am the navigator. And when I am not in that element I am a bit like, "What are you looking at? Why are you staring at me?" It's embarrassing.

SB: Children love laughing?

MJ: I think we are going to find out in this next century that there is something really magical about laughter. Whenever I feel real depressed and down and out, I force myself to laugh and I try to think of something funny and I feel better. I think some kind of chemical reaction takes place in the soul. I really feel better and I force myself to smile. I think just smiling, the muscles, it does something and I feel a lot better. I saw Prince smile for the first time and my little cousin was there and he was making little noises and he smiled, and it was the most heartwarming thing to see my son smile. He had just come from the hospital. He was two days old. My eyes watered, which is sweet because he was responding and there was a contact going on between the two of them. I thought it was beautiful. I love that. Oh G-d, do I love to laugh.

SB: You didn't have the freedom a lot of children have. You missed a lot of that freedom. Do you feel freer when you laugh?

MJ: Yes, I feel free. I feel like I am beginning to be normal. I love to play. Even though I am very serious when I work, very, very serious, I am constantly playing. Also, I can't help it. I have every kind of toy and water gun. . . . One of the ways I handle pressure is I like to play and climb trees. I love climbing trees.

SB: You have that tree house at Neverland.

MJ: By the water. I love to hear the water. It is complete therapy for me. I go up there all the time and sit there and create and I write songs up there.

SB: Does your Neverland staff know you are up there?

MJ: They see me climbing up there sometimes. Sometimes when they can't find me anywhere they say, "He must be climbing up a tree." They call up to the tree, "You have a phone call!" I have to come down. Some people say you ought to put a phone up there. I say, "I don't want to put a phone in the tree. That's my chance to get away from phones."

SB: What are the things that really make you laugh? Do children make you laugh more than adults?

MJ: To Prince [who is with us]: "Prince, what makes Daddy laugh?"

Prince: Three Stooges.

MJ: He's right. I love them. The fat one . . . I scream with laughter. I keep the Three Stooges with me wherever I go. It makes me happy. I have watched them all my life.

SB: What is it about them? Is it the fact that they can, like, hurt each other and no one gets hurt and everything's funny?

MJ: Yeah, Curly is the killer. Remember Curly—the fat one, right, Prince? [Prince starts jumping around, imitating Curly.] Yeah, he loves it, too. I love them.

SB: That's what makes you laugh out loud?

MJ: Yeah, I scream. I scream, I keep the Three Stooges with me wherever I go. It makes me happy. I love them. I've watched them all my life.

> *[Kids] remind us to stay happy.*
> *Hang on, stay happy, be like them.*

SB: The best kind of comedy is like the Three Stooges?

MJ: I love the Three Stooges. I am crazy about them. That's what I like about kids. They laugh all the time. They find an excuse to laugh about something. They are always in bliss. They remind us to stay happy. Hang on, stay happy, be like them.

Imagination

Our minds create our world.

SB: So our bodies are limited, but our imagination, our minds are unlimited. And once we close it off, we cease to be infinite.

MJ: Yes, and our minds create our world. Our thought processes create what we get in life and become. We just forget. I am not saying we just forget. We are created in His image and if you are created in my image, it's like looking in the mirror. Aren't you part of the image?

SB: But human beings forget that. Does the imagination help remind us of it? The very infinite quality of imagination is what reminds us of its divine nature?

MJ: Yes, because imagination is unlimited, so we can go anywhere, do anything, and become anything, be anything, see anything, at any time we want. That is a very powerful medium. That's a very dangerous medium.

You know all the great things that come out of childhood. Did you know that the Wright brothers had this dream of flying when they were children? Didn't Edison start being an inventor when he was in his boyhood? And Lincoln dreamed of being a great lawyer or president when he was just a child? Spielberg, when he was eight or nine, started making these movies and dreaming of being a big Hollywood director. It came out of that childlike imagination, that unlimited imagination. Children have the greatest imagination. They don't know what they can't do yet. Now, where we are just getting to in our society, where popular culture is and icons are, our kids thought of it years ago.

Directors like Spielberg and Lucas, they just hang around children and get the idea from kids. [They'll say to a kid] "What are you now?" "I am a giant monster and they are trying to capture me and . . ." They see it, it's real. Even their imaginary world is real. If you step on their imaginary friend, they cry. "You killed my friend. How

> *Imagination is unlimited, so we can go anywhere, do anything, and become anything, be anything, see anything, at any time we want. That is a very powerful medium.*

could you kill him?" They have created this real world, and to go into that world with them and really become a part of it is the most magical thing in the world. I love it. It's where I live. Adults lose it. It has become my place of refuge, my hiding place, that whole place where they live. I hate saying "we." I don't want to be like them. They end up forgetting. Coming back to that is to have paradise regained.

SB: Is the world of imagination important because it is important to imagine things that aren't? Or is it important because if we imagine these things, then we can make them real? In other words, is the imagination only important because it can affect the real world, or even without the real world, it is important to have an imagination?

MJ: I think imagination is important for the inner self and the soul. It's important for the brain. It's G-d telling us . . . we are bigger than anything. We are the universe.

SB: Are you bored by people without imagination?

MJ: Yes. I am hurt by them because they don't realize who they are. It is like taking a computer with no instructions on the keys and pressing, going, "This thing is boring. I don't know what to do with it." When we are born, we don't have instructions. *We* are more amazing than a computer. We are born without instructions. We don't know that this thing is unbelievable and dangerous, too.

SB: Most adults would say they like being around their own children. It's other people's children that they don't want to be around. They want to be around adults. "I want to talk football, politics." And what you are saying is that these "adult" subjects are boring. When I am around children I feel an expansiveness in their universe. It's not constrained like an adult's world. An adult's world is too limited. I'd rather be in a world that's big, a kid's world. You feel constrained in the adult world because it lacks imagination. You feel jailed by it.

MJ: Adults who have the big imagination are the most childlike. If you hang around them, like I know Spielberg and

Lucas and creative people, [Francis Ford] Coppola, they are very much like children. They believe they are Peter Pan.

SB: Their imaginations can fly. They refuse to accept what can't be done.

MJ: I still have dreams about flying, and I wake up very upset because I thought I was flying in my dreams and I knew it was possible and I really thought I was soaring.

SB: But even in a waking state you can fly in your imagination. Wasn't it Einstein who said something like we only use 5 percent of our minds, and about 95 percent remains undeveloped. Well, you know, Steve Jobs, who founded

> *Adults who have the big imagination are the most childlike.*

Apple computer, later came up with this computer called Next, about ten years ago. I used one, an amazing machine. It was ten years ahead of its competition and no one could understand how he had built it and they asked his friend, "How does he come up with these innovations?" The friend said, "Well, all of his competitors went to college and studied engineering. They know what can be done. Steve dropped out of college. So he doesn't know what can't be done." Knowledge can be limiting.

MJ: He's like a little kid.

Jealousy, Envy, and Admiration

Never jealous ... complete admiration. ...
Complete inspiration, never jealousy.

MJ: Do you believe that story of the Garden of Eden?

SB: Yes.

MJ: Do you believe that Cain and Abel were a bad son and a good son? Well, where did he learn the bad from?

SB: The bad was desire. Cain perceived his brother to be more beloved of G-d, more precious to his Creator, than he himself was. And rather than lift himself up and better himself, he took the easier way out and eliminated the competition. You told me once about your brother. You love each other and then suddenly you were really successful and his career was not going as well. He had two choices. He could say, "G-d has a plan and Michael is part of a divine plan in inspiring people with music and art, and I probably have a place within it as well. I am not going to be jealous. I am going to find my place. I am very happy for Michael. In fact, Michael's success inspires me to find my place, what I am good at, the contribution I can make."

Instead a brother can decide, "No. I want to have what *he* has." Instead of saying, "You know, I am going to do something in my own way and become the beloved of G-d," he can focus on having what belongs to his brother.

It is what I say is the difference between jealousy and envy. Jealousy is not a bad thing. We think jealousy is a bad emotion. If Prince called someone else "Daddy" it would hurt you because he is your son. So you have a legitimate right to feel jealous about something like that. You have a right to be possessive because he is your child. In the same way that if you gave other children more affection than Paris, she would feel bad because you are her daddy. Jealousy is not a bad emotion. Jealousy is an act of possessiveness to claim what is rightly yours.

The problem is not jealousy, but envy. Envy is where you want to have that which belongs to somebody else. So jealousy makes us zealously guard the integrity of our relationships. Envy makes us desire someone else's possessions or relationships and live permanently lusting after that which is not ours.

You often say that a lot of the attacks you have experienced have been out of jealousy. Is that specifically an adult thing? Do children never show jealousy? Are Prince and Paris jealous if you have ever shown too much affection for another child?

MJ: Well, Prince knows how I feel about other children. He knows how much I love children. He wrote me a letter that said, "Baby? Show me the baby?" because I always call them babies and he knows how I feel.

SB: Did any child ever come to Neverland and say, "Hey. This isn't fair. Look at all these things that Prince and Paris have. They even have their own amusement park." If you brought kids to Neverland would they never look at Prince and Paris and say, "Hey, look at the life that you have. We don't have this life"? Because you have been the victim of jealousy throughout your life.

MJ: Serious. Oh boy, that's a tough one.

SB: You have probably seen jealousy in how children relate to you.

MJ: Oh yeah!

SB: If you give too much affection to one.

MJ: I am the perfect example in that area because I have seen how they want to say, "I'm sitting next to him." "No, I am. Get out of the way." That happens all the time. I don't know if they have been taught to be that way by their parents. I think when I show certain children a lot of attention and they are with me, like a family, and they are with me all the time alone, this whole family, then if there is another family who comes over with some other kids, then they start to feel that they are being edged out by the others and I explain to them how that could just never happen. That they must be loving and giving to everybody. Once I explain it to them they have been fine afterwards.

SB: What you seem to be saying is that children can cure themselves of jealousy if you explain to them, "Look, it's okay. I'm still your friend. I love you and want to be close to you."

MJ: Children have the ability to become jealous. But if you explain it to them, it is like a clean new slate. You can mold and shape the way you want them to be.

SB: Then it's both nature and nurture? Children have a certain nature but you can help by reinforcing behaviors?

MJ: You take those same kids, who were in Columbine [Eric Harris and Dylan Klebold]. If I had raised them they would be two different kids. They wouldn't be anything like what happened to them later on in their lives because of nurturing, bringing out the best of what G-d gave

> *Children have the ability to become jealous.*
> *But if you explain it to them, it is like a clean new slate.*

them, letting that take shape and form, that would have never happened. The way I look at them and say, "I love you," and spend time and hold them and kiss them on the head and the cheek. No way, they were not given attention and affection and love. They were off doing their own thing. No way. I think we are the product of our environment and our upbringing and people have to bring out the best in us instead of bringing out the horrible qualities.

SB: That would mean, Michael, that in kids there is the really good but there is the potential for evil.

MJ: There is also the potential. Yes, there is.

SB: The job of the parent is not to give the kid the goodness but to bring it like flowers growing out of the ground. The potential for growth is there. You just have to provide the water and care?

MJ: That's true. I really believe it. I don't believe there is such a thing as a bad seed.

SB: Do you remember anyone you thought was bad?

MJ: No. Father Flanagan, who built Boys Town—I think it was in Nebraska—he said, "There is no such thing as a bad boy or girl." I believe that. With love and nurturing and care and the right, proper [upbringing] . . .

SB: But if we don't give them that guidance, then the bad stuff can come out because then they start to get envious feelings. They are deprived, neglected.

MJ: Well, what happened to the good kid who was the good son who suddenly goes astray and becomes imprisoned later in life? He meets up with a bad friend, a bad influence. That could easily happen.

SB: Will you try and protect Prince and Paris from bad influences, including children who you think might be a bad influence?

MJ: Absolutely, because the children can be influenced by another bad child or another bad parent, a bad upbringing.

SB: Does jealousy have no role? Were you never jealous, envious, of someone in your career who made you work harder?

MJ: Never jealous. Admiration, complete admiration.

SB: So admiration can bring even greater goals than jealousy because it is positive and not negative. So you would look at Fred Astaire and say, "I want to be able to do that."

MJ: Yes, absolutely. Complete inspiration, never jealousy. It's wrong, but people are like that, Shmuley, aren't they? It's true? Can't people look at somebody great and get totally jealous of them?

SB: Sure, but you have never felt that?

MJ: I don't understand a person who could do that.

SB: For you it has always been inspiration? You have been in awe and wonder of those with great talent?

MJ: Can a person become jealous of G-d?

SB: Sure. Look at Stalin and Hitler. They tried to be G-d. They wanted to decide life and death.

MJ: Wow.

SB: Because they lose the sense of awe and wonder. G-d doesn't impress them. He threatens them. They want to be all-powerful, so they can't submit to G-d's authority. They become enemies of G-d.

Joy

*Children come with the
quintessence of bliss.*

SB: Can adults learn joy from children?

MJ: Children come with the quintessence of bliss. You feel it in their smile and the light in their eyes. When they come into the room you can feel them beaming, I can feel that. I could scream. Before every concert they bring the kids to me. I have to see them before I go out, and my security knows that. To me it is like a B12 shot. I am ready to conquer the world now. I just got reminded about what this is all about. They inject it into me. I am ready to take on the universe. It's true. I did all of my albums for kids. It was my gift back. Thank you, thank you, thank you. Everything is for them. The greatest of joy.

SB: Most children are happy, yet so many adults are not happy. What's the lesson we can learn from kids about joy? Is it that they are joyous so we should be joyous, or is it that they are joyous with almost nothing. They don't need a cause to make them happy. They're always playing. It is not about possessions and fame, they are just happy. Before a concert you want to put on a good show for your fans. You are a star and you want to be good. Is being around kids like saying, "Look, I am not doing this to impress anybody. Kids are joyous. I am going to be joyous. I am just going to be." Is it that you felt less judged? Is that part of the joy as well, that kids are joyous because they have nothing to prove? Adults have so many pressures . . . you live with phenomenal pressures. Does that take away joy?

MJ: Well, they don't have all the responsibilities and the pressures and all the things that we have to do and think about. They are just free. It's like taking a fawn and saying, "Go." Mother says, "Go, run to the forest. Go." And you run and see the trees and the sky and the clouds and there's a butterfly. They just want to play and they are caught up in this world of fun. Their G-d is fun. They worship fun. So they have this clean slate and this whole lot of different things to do. That's how they are all the time. The world is gift-wrapped for them and everything is a new experience and they know that it is all out there waiting for them and all these different categories of fun, a wonderful fantastical mission to take. Why do they lose it? Why does it go away? You felt that way, you remember feeling that way. Can you go back to that place?

SB: The only time I've felt like that again is when I was with you watching *Toy Story* on Thanksgiving, and at Neverland, when we went to the tree that morning. We climbed up and spent a full hour there, just hanging out. And I have to say, it was pretty liberating. Two grown men, hanging out in a tree house. It was memorable.

MJ: Isn't that wonderful? Everybody should have that experience and never feel that I am too grown up to climb a tree.

SB: Is that part of children's joy as well, that they are closer to nature? When we draw closer to artificial things we can't be as joyous?

MJ: Yes. A child can pick up a leaf and be fascinated by it, or stare at a butterfly's wings. A grown-up will go, "It's just a butterfly," but it's not. It's a miracle. It's an evolution of nature and you can trace how that happens. The kids are right. It is awe-inspiring. The way it reflects in the sun and the colors and what it all means and how it all started.

> *What is happening in the universe is always happening in this drop of water. It's all a miracle and it's all amazing and we can never rest our senses or grow dull of finding curiosity in the world, of knowing that there is a whole world of things to experience.*

Everything is fascinating to me. From a drop of water and how a whole colony of species lives in there and everything is amazing. What is happening in the universe is always happening in this drop of water. It's all a miracle and it's all amazing and we can never rest our senses or grow dull of finding curiosity in the world, of knowing that there is a whole world of things to experience.

That's what is so phenomenal now. That grown-ups are just knocking wood and finding out about computers and the Internet and the way they feel when the whole world is at their disposal right there and they go, "Oh, I could go anywhere and do anything on this thing." Kids feel that way every day without a computer. That's how they wake up in the morning, feeling just like that and feeling more so. Wherever I want to go, I can go. It's great. That's how kids feel. They are that excited.

Love
and
Guidance

You can't overdose on love.

SB: One of the most powerful things you have said to me is that at the beginning of all knowledge is the knowledge that you are loved. No matter who you are or where you come from, you have to know that you are loved. You say the single most important thing to heal the world is to first and foremost give children unconditional love.

MJ: Unconditional love is all you have. You can't overdose on love, you never can. It's a beautiful thing.

SB: Major studies show that children who experience no tactility bear emotional scars that will not heal later in life. Even if you survived the Holocaust, your body can recover later in life. [I used this example because I had just introduced Michael to Elie Wiesel, the Nobel Peace Prize laureate and Holocaust survivor.] But if you are not shown love in life, you will not recover. You will be cynical, even when you're older. You'll be untrusting. In thinking about your own love and parenting of your children, how would you describe the ideal parent-child relationship?

MJ: Mmmm, respect, honesty. I should put love first. Love, respect, and honesty. Being totally open about everything. That's the closest thing you can have.

SB: In raising Prince and Paris, has your parenting been based on those three principles: love, respect, and honesty? You never lie to them? You don't even bend the truth? . . . You know one of the greatest rabbis, the Lubavitcher Rebbe, Rabbi Menachem Schneerson, my spiritual mentor, always said, "If you lie to children they will never trust you again."

But what happens when you have to discipline children? Children are born with the potential for goodness, but parents must impart values to them. Without a loving parent who is also strict on discipline, it may never come

> *You have to discipline them without anger.*
> *That's the first important thing I would tell any parent.*
> *If you do it with anger, if you hurt them, you will*
> *say to yourself, "What did I do?"*

out, like if you had to discipline Prince and Paris, because a child still has to know that "No" is "No!" And there are certain things that they cannot do.

MJ: You have to discipline them without anger. That's the first important thing I would tell any parent. If you do it with anger, if you hurt them, you will say to yourself, "What did I do?"

If Prince or Paris does something naughty or bad, I take something away and it breaks their heart. But you have to discipline them. I asked Elizabeth [Taylor] what was the height of her discipline. She said she'd speak to them harshly and if they did something very bad, "I would lay them on my knee and give them a hard whack on the bottom." I can't do that. If I hit them and they cried, that would kill me, knowing that they cried from pain that I inflicted on them. I'm against hitting kids. Even though there are kids in school who get away with saying F U to the teachers. Something's got to be done, but not that. I couldn't do that [hit a child]. I can see them cry because they have to go to the corner, which is where they're sent if they're naughty.

> *My biggest dream is one day for Prince and Paris to say to somebody, "He was the best dad." I would just start crying, just weeping, that's my reward.*

SB: One of your main principles as a parent is that you never want your children to be afraid.

MJ: Never. I think before anyone should discipline their child they should stop a second, take a deep breath, do a silent prayer. Do that and then chastise them in as loving a way as you can. Don't do it with anger. If you do it with anger, you're sorry, it hurts too much. It's the wrong way to do it.

SB: Do you feel that you were shown anger unnecessarily as a child?

MJ: Yes. Ahhhaaa. Absolutely. My biggest dream is one day for Prince and Paris to say to somebody, "He was the best dad." I would just start crying, just weeping, that's my re-ward. That's all I want is to say, "He was the best dad." We'd go there, we would do this. You know? That's all I want back.

SB: When people get older, like you said about your father, they want to be close to their children.

MJ: Yeah.

SB: I mean it's a circle. You start as a child and you sort of end as a child. You become a bit more innocent.

MJ: Why can't they see that earlier, though?

SB: And after everything you went through with your father, how do you try and compensate now with Prince and Paris?

MJ: I overcompensate. If I see a mother in a movie, and she's acting and I see her slap her son, I run out of the room and I cry. I can't take it. I have seen situations where they shake the child really badly . . . it conjures up a lot of my past and my childhood and I can't take it.

SB: You want to give Prince and Paris the unconditional love that is going to make sure they grow up knowing what-ever they do that there is a strong character, a father, who loved them with his heart and his soul?

MJ: Oh, they know already. They are just little kids and they say certain things that are kinda unusual for little kids. They will keep hugging me over some little thing I gave them over two weeks ago, which is sweet. "Thank you for that little bunny you gave me." I say, "Prince, that was a week ago. You're welcome." They keep doing this, which is sweet. It's love.

SB: All I want from my kids, I always tell them I want two things. I want you to love G-d and I want you to love His children. That's it. Success and everything else are completely subordinate to those two essential things. But you said whether or not Prince and Paris duplicate your success or anything it's not what's important to you. What do you most want for them?

MJ: If they're successful I would be very happy, you know, at what they do. And I hope it's in the arts, but they have to choose their own profession. I just want them to . . . I want to be successful in being a great father. I want them to say, "We felt completely loved and he was, like, incredible." I want to represent what I want fathers to be with their children.

SB: But you realize that by doing that, to an extent, you may ensure that they don't really succeed professionally, because if Prince feels loved and nurtured and secure, he won't have to prove himself to the world to the same extent that you have. You've said to me once that you're a perfectionist because you're always trying to prove yourself to your own father.

MJ: Yeah.

SB: If Prince feels love, he'll just be happy being a lawyer somewhere or an accountant, and he'll come home and he'll run to his kids and his wife will love him. It will be great. You don't need all that, and you're happy to live with that? You don't have the public adulation? The thousands of screaming fans?

MJ: If that is completely true, yeah, I want them to be good people. But I would love to see them be successful at something in the arts, you know?

SB: That's your great love?

MJ: Oh G-d.

SB: Do you try to protect them from growing up too fast? We were talking about kids' rush to become adults, almost as if they are embarrassed to be children. In traditional Jewish circles like ours, kids stay at home usually until they get married, and they marry young. When do you think kids should move out?

MJ: I think kids leave home much too early. I did something that was bad. I'm a natural tenor but I used to force my voice to go higher because I never wanted to grow up. I always wanted to sound like a kid. And when I won my Grammy Award for *Thriller*, if you listen to me speak, I sound like a kid, and that's when all the jokes and the teasing began and people imitating me. Then I got to the point where I decided, no, I'm just going to talk like me. And when I started talking like me, I couldn't sing in the key I used to sing in, so I sing lower now. I just wanted to be a kid.

SB: So even though you were the biggest star in the world, and people were sleeping outside your parents' gate the whole time, you were still leading a normal life at home with your parents because you thought it was appropriate for you to be at home?

MJ: Yeah, it was natural to me. I wasn't ready for the world yet, and I was very naïve. My parents wanted me around. Maybe it was unusual in some ways. We didn't have dinner together. It was eat and run because we were a working, show-business family. I had special cooks, Sikhs in a turban, to make vegetarian food for me. But otherwise, you know, I'd watch lots of cartoons. It was a lovely big house with three acres of gardens and a candy store where you could make your own ice creams and a flower shop and English Tudor garden, a movie theater, a big recording studio.

SB: What about the fact that children are sometimes nasty to one another? You sometimes see children who need to be taught to share and they are sometimes nasty. Bullying is something that children often do. There is a kid on the bus who bullies one of my daughters so much and has been so mean to her. His parents have talked to him and he denied bullying her. He said, "I would never do that." I complained to the principal of the school, but he still does it. My daughter comes home and cries.

MJ: How old is the kid who bullies her?

SB: Twelve, and she is eleven, a pure soul. All kids are pure but she is extremely pure. She is a pure soul and she doesn't know how to fight back. It could be that these children who bully didn't have enough love. They were corrupted. They are exhibiting adult qualities, but your theory would be that if this kid who bullies her had been shown unconditional love by his parents, he wouldn't need to do this and he wouldn't be in so much pain.

MJ: I believe they do it for attention. I think you could trace every evil in adults to when they were growing up. We have to be so careful and love and be loving all the time. You don't know how you are hurting them later on in every little incident. I read their eyes and find out who is

> *We have to be so careful and love and be loving all the time. You don't know how you are hurting [children] later on in every little incident.*

hurting the most and give them the longest hug, or I pick the fattest or the most grotesque-looking and people will say, "Why did you pick that one?" and I'll say, "This is the one who needed it the most." You can tell because they are looking sad and they don't think you are going to like them. They are afraid of looking at you sometimes because they have been teased so much. You can tell . . . a beat dog acts differently.

We had a dog, her name was Black Girl, and she was half wolf and half German shepherd. My father is a hunter and he loves hunting and he loves guns. I'm the opposite.

I hate hunting and I hate guns. One day he was polishing his rifle and the dog would go, "Eh uh, eh [whimpering noise]," backing up like that, and he goes, "Kids, look at this." So he took the gun and aimed it at the dog and the dog went running under the bed and he was wondering, how did the dog know? We checked and found that the dog had been abused, and a hunter had owned the dog and they used to shoot at him as he was in the wild and the dog knew what a gun looked like and what it sounds like. So whenever someone in the neighborhood, like at New Year's, would be shooting their gun, this German shepherd would run and hide and cry. I realized this German shepherd had problems conditioned and that's the same thing with all of us, isn't it? Right? We gave this dog a lot of love and hugs and kisses.

SB: Could you undo the fear?

MJ: We sure worked hard, between Janet and myself, who loved this dog. We gave her a lot of love and she did a lot better. But then there were those who would come over and ruin it for us.

SB: All the mean-spiritedness that you have felt, have you ever wanted to hate people back?

MJ: No. As a response to very mean journalists who just lie, your response is not "I hate you for what you wrote," but rather, "I don't understand why you did this to me and I will leave it like that." It hurts very much because they think you are made out of some strong kind of substance and that you can rise above it all the time. But you try to find a way to keep your head above it and it is not always like that because it does hurt.

SB: But you have never wanted to hate back?

MJ: No.

SB: Because you would lose that childlike innocence.

MJ: Yes, I never want to hate back.

SB: But what does the average child do, Michael? Do they start hating back, do you think? Let's say someone was mean to Prince and then Prince yelled at him. What would you say to him? How would you react if Prince showed

> *Like Gandhi said, "An eye for an eye and the whole world goes blind."*

anger back? And let's say Prince was right. Someone had been mean to him. Would you be happy that Prince had learned to defend himself, or would you feel, "No, I don't want that from you."

MJ: I'd prefer if he could understand why the other person was taking offense and try to reach their hearts, that's what I would do. Like Gandhi said, "An eye for an eye and the whole world goes blind." You can't be like that. It is just creating more friction. I am very protective of all children. If I see someone hurting a child in any way, I realize I have a problem with it. If I see it in a movie and I know they are acting, I have to leave and give a good cry, or I get real angry, and then I go back in. If I am watching a movie and I see someone slap a child real hard and he cries, I really can't take it. I learned that about myself. It hits a nerve and I can relate to it because it happened to me a lot.

When my father used to . . . he had a horrible way of disciplining you. He looked at you like this and said, "Come here," and you knew what that meant. He would slap you real hard and his prints would be on your face, and he would push you and shove you in front of the fans, crying with tears in your eyes. To discipline and to shame are two different things, you don't cross that line to shame. That hurt me very much and I don't know if he realized it.

SB: So if Prince and Paris did something wrong, you would discipline them but never shame them?

MJ: Never shame them.

SB: So you would say, "Prince, that was wrong."

MJ: You would talk about it and make them understand. You don't shame them, no way. That's wrong.

SB: Do you think that even children have a sense of their own dignity, not just adults?

MJ: Yeah. You don't shame them ever in front of their friends. Ever. Ever. Ever. They will never forget it if you do.

SB: So based on what you are saying, do you feel at all fearful of being an adult in the sense that adults can inflict pain, that they can show anger? Is that something you have

never wanted to be? Is that one of the reasons that you in-
sist on remaining childlike, because you're concerned
about developing adult aggression?

MJ: I never want to be that. I am not proud of being an adult.
I don't like saying it. I never even say it.

SB: Let me ask you this. Prince and Paris and all kids are
sometimes naughty. What about when children are cruel
and bully each other? First of all, where does that come
from? And second, what can we do about it?

MJ: I think it is from a lack of love and attention and respect.

> *People don't talk to their children. They ignore them.*
> *That's why children go out and do those things*
> *for attention, and they hurt others and don't realize it.*

SB: What should parents do about it, should they reprimand
them or show them extra love?

MJ: Give them more love, hold them, touch them. Look in
their eyes and talk to them. People don't talk to their children. They ignore them. That's why children go out and
do those things for attention, and they hurt others and
don't realize it.

SB: But you would say that if children were shown the love
and attention they need, they would never behave that
way? So Sigmund Freud, who said that children are nar-
cissistic, they are selfish and self-centered . . .

MJ: He was wrong. Wrong.

SB: What about the fact that children can be possessive about their toys? One of their first words is "mine." Even children who are shown immense amounts of love say "mine."

MJ: That's true. Even the ones who are shown a lot of love say "mine."

SB: Seems so. You show Prince and Paris an immense amount of love. Do they say "mine"?

MJ: To each other, but not to other kids.

SB: That's because you consciously teach them that it is not "mine."

MJ: It is important to share.

SB: What about your own sense of value and self-esteem? Perhaps one of the strongest arguments we're discussing is that when children are not shown unconditional love, they begin to devalue themselves. They feel like they don't matter. They don't have enough self-esteem. They don't think enough of themselves. You weren't given all that love. How do you deal with issues of self-esteem?

MJ: I try to think about where I compensated for a lot of the loss myself. I can't quite find it sometimes. I think that is part of the gift I have, that I went through a lot and was able to come out of it and become a better person. That's why I feel I suffered and lost a lot of childhood issues and values, because it's made me so sensitive to children now. It is unbelievable how I am with them, really. That's why I think it was meant to be, that's all I can say.

SB: So children are the compensation?

MJ: I think so. They are my teachers. I watch them and I learn. It is important for us to try and be like them and imitate them. They are golden.

SB: You never had the experience as a child of being tucked in and loved, of being shown unconditional love? You didn't have that. But you had fans who showed you love, though maybe it was based on your performance, rather than your essence.

MJ: The fans know me and they know my heart. They have giant pictures of babies and big cutouts of children holding hands and they bring kids and they know I love them. And they have given me awards and things, acknowledging me as a person other than a celebrity and how they care about issues with kids and stuff like that. Oh boy. One day people will get it. They'll understand. I think it is the way G-d wants us to be.

SB: It is easy for you to be innocent because even when people attack you, you can retreat to this beautiful ranch that you have. So you don't have to claw back. You are very successful, so you can afford to forgive people and remain childlike. "But me?" someone can say, "I live in a trailer park. How can I forgive people? Life is bitter for me. G-d has let me down. I have no time for my children. I am a single mother with two jobs to support my kids." What would you say to someone who says, "Come on, Michael. This is not realistic. You want me to be like Peter Pan? You want to take me to this fantasy land called Neverland. Get real. I can't go to a fantasy land. I have children to support. My husband beats me." What would you say to someone like that?

MJ: I would think they should try to find the truth about the power of love, and the way that I think it should be done, without sounding selfish, the way I have discovered what real bliss is. I think if they even gave it a chance they would feel it.

SB: Is there freedom where you are right now? Is there freedom in holding on to a childlike way of being? Do you feel like all the adults are in prison somewhere and you are the only free one?

MJ: Aha. Yes. I don't know how anybody wouldn't love it. It's the best.

SB: If we could walk right into the Norman Rockwell painting, is that the kind of world you would like to inhabit? Is that the kind of world you would like to help create?

MJ: Oh yeah.

SB: You are a single parent raising your children. The one thing that people agree on is the need ideally to have both parents involved in raising a child. Will your children suffer from only having one parent raise them? Or do you believe that you're going to be able to compensate with enough love for two parents?

MJ: Yeah, or one half who doesn't really want them. If you truly unconditionally love them with all you have, you deserve to raise them by yourself. That's all they need. It's love.

SB: So you believe it is not a question of numbers. One person can give it to them as long as the love is unconditional.

MJ: Absolutely.

Openness and Vulnerability

I love how a child is so honest.

play games. It's all the stuff we talked about before.
put up all these mental barricades, pretending not
eed . . . it's psychological warfare.
cherish our independence. But kids aren't afraid to
on to Mommy's dress and cling to her, and they are
afraid to show need. Can we learn neediness from
dren? Do you think children teach adults not to be
d to be needy?
ourse they do.

> ink adults mask their needs. . . . They condition
> selves to put up barricades and use psychology,
> like, "I don't need you." But in truth they
> are hiding, they play games.

, love and fear are opposites. The quintessential pos-
of love is to extend yourself, to expose your soft un-
elly. When you hug someone you literally create a
within yourself for someone else to exist. You make
self vulnerable. But the quintessential posture of fear
very opposite. It's to draw in your extremities, to
in your arms and your legs to protect your torso.
love you expand, but with fear you contract, you de-
back to an embryonic state.
ow are you going to teach Prince and Paris acceptance
you also have to teach them to be wary?

SB: What you seem to be describing to me is that creativity involves freedom. Unlike adults, who have to submit to pressure, children are really free. They say whatever they want. They do whatever they want, and they are not intimidated. Adults are almost like prisoners. They are almost jailed in the social constraints and expectations that are imposed on them.

MJ: Yeah, they are trying to be what society expects of them, and children are just happy, whimsical, and fun-loving.

> [Children] have this excitement, this glow in their eye.

They have this excitement, this glow in their eye, and I have been in situations in meetings with a bunch of lawyers and sometimes a kid will come in the room and they will keep talking. And I make everybody stop and they all have to say, "Hello," or show respect, to make the kid feel special. And the lawyers don't get it. To me, G-d just walked into the room and we have to show respect.

I love how a child is so honest. If they are jealous, they will tell you. If they are mad at you, they'll tell you . . . "You like him more than me." Adults won't say that. They will be vindictive and find another way to hurt you because of their jealousy.

SB: They have to overtly hide or mask their jealousy.

MJ: Yeah. Yeah. I just love it because there is a natural G-dliness about them. They love being together. One child who has never met another before will be friends within two seconds and start talking to each other. You cannot get grown-ups to do that. If you take babies and you put them in a bed and you spread them out when they are sleeping, within the hour, subconsciously, in the alpha state or something, they will find a way to huddle up together. Puppies do it, kittens do it, and children do it. They find a way. They end up right next to each other and it's so sweet. They find each other in their sleep. But we, we are busy trying to set barriers and barricades. "You sit over there, and you sit over there." That's the sad part, isn't it?

SB: Children have none of those prejudices, none of those barriers. So when you meet a child, you're saying, there is instant familiarity. You don't have to work on friendship or kinship. Whereas with adults, initially there is a bit of awkwardness and you have to start trusting each other because the natural state is to distrust.

MJ: The children just open up to me.

SB: But what if someone were to say to you that this isn't real, that the world is an awful place and you have to get out of Neverland because it is an illusion, a fantasy world? What

if someone were to say, "Mi
you say about children, but
you just have to get used to
and people are mean. And i
you are that much more vu
you are just going to open y
pain and attack and hurt.'
state you have retained? A
warrior, he protects himse
cided not to do that. You
and you decided to protec
you regret it at all?

MJ: Do I regret being the way I

SB: Even though you say that
Even though people can th

MJ: There is such beauty and g
what I do. All the ideas st
conjuring up great thought

SB: You say, "I need the childre
children." You are not afra
"need" is a four-letter wor
most adults it expresses de
I 'need'?"

MJ: I think adults mask their
and they have their mates
dition themselves to put
ogy, like, "I don't need you

they
The
to n

SB: We
hold
not
chil
afra

MJ: Of

I th
ther

SB: Now
ture
derb
spac
your
is th
brin
With
volv
H
wher

MJ: There's a fine line. But I don't want to teach them to judge people, "Oh, he looks like he is going to hurt me." It's tough. I want them to be street-smart. I think it is *my* job to judge for them. My job.

SB: One of the parental responsibilities to ensure that you don't corrupt your kids is to protect them so that they don't have to protect themselves. You can do it for them. But only for a while. Later, they're going to have to learn how to protect themselves. Most parents would teach the kid, "If you see this kind of person, you should stay away from them." You've decided to let them love everybody and it's your job to protect them.

MJ: Absolutely. I believe that.

SB: That's a very important lesson for all parents, Michael. I also don't want to teach my children fear.

MJ: That's what has hurt a lot of our children, putting them in a situation where they start to become judgmental or prejudiced about the way they dress or have their hair, and it's not true. Parents shouldn't do that to them, they should let them just see what happens. . . . When kids come out, I have seen the toughest, worst people let their guards down because the light has come into the room.

SB: So children teach us acceptance, not only mentally but experientially.

MJ: Absolutely.

SB: Do you feel more free around children? For example, you said that being a celebrity, you don't get your own life and people take pictures of you and you can't walk in the street and you have to wear a disguise. Do you feel freer around kids, more natural, more liberated?

MJ: Not only do I feel free, but I feel like I am standing in the face of G-d. I feel honored, that I am the lucky one. That G-d has blessed you to be in their presence, and other people don't get it because they treat them like they are just throwaway. I just come in the room and there is this sense of bliss. You can feel it, you can touch it, and it's evoking from them because it is consciousness is what it is, spirituality.

SB: Is it healing for you?

MJ: It saved my life.

SB: It takes away the pain when you are in the presence of kids?

MJ: It saves my life.

SB: So if G-d is light, to use that metaphor, whereas adults build these barriers that block off the light and they get dark, children are translucent, with no conscious barriers between them and the light. G-d's light shines through them unobstructed.

MJ: They are the light. I was telling Frank the other day, in my opinion Gavin represents the white light we see before we die, that hope that comes. [Gavin was the boy stricken with cancer whom Michael had hosted, along with his family, at Neverland. He was the child who would later become Michael's 2003 accuser. Michael was acquitted on all charges.] Don't be afraid, he's like an angel. How could he not be sweet and kind in his soul? There is a message there somewhere, the kids have it.

SB: But you are able to be yourself and in that sense you are freer about kids, as you have said, you don't put up all these barriers.

MJ: I feel the most freedom when I am with them.

SB: Okay, another thing we learn from children is transparency. Unlike adults, children are transparent. They're

> *When kids come out, I have seen the toughest, worst people let their guards down because the light has come into the room.*

not cagey about what they want. It's like they are made of glass. You can see right through them.

MJ: I can see right through them. I communicate with them in silence. Looking in the eyes, I can feel exactly what they are saying, as soon as they look at me, as soon as we have eye contact it's done, because telepathy is real strong with children, you can feel it. They are readers from in the cradle. They can see when you are not happy. They read expressions staring in your eyes. We don't have to say that much. We can do it with expression. But they are in that place where they can feel emotions so much stronger than adults. Very telepathic. They are much more in tune with the whole universe.

SB: If you see the world through a child's eyes, what would you say it looks like?

MJ: It is gift-wrapped. It is magic. It is wonderment. It is wonderful and you are curious about everything. It is fantastical. It is great. It is awe-inspiring.

SB: When you see that gift-wrapped world, do you see any of the ugliness of the world? Do you see things that hurt you as well? You see a lot of people who are mean. How do you deal with that?

> *[Children] are in that place where they can feel emotions so much stronger than adults. Very telepathic. They are much more in tune with the whole universe.*

MJ: I don't understand it. I don't understand it.

SB: And you think that as long as you don't understand it, that means that you don't have to change to accommodate it? It's not like you say to yourself, "I have to get defensive." Rather, you just say to yourself, "I am just going to say I don't understand . . . this shouldn't be." To you it remains a mystery, and if it's a mystery, if it remains irrational, then it can't invade your own personality. It can't penetrate your psyche. It can't affect you.

MJ: Yes.

SB: So if you meet someone who is mean, how do you react if you are looking through the eyes of a child?

MJ: It hurts. When I was little, Bill Cosby used to see me in the hallway of the NBC studios and say [raises and hardens voice], "Hey, what are you kids doing in here? Get these kids outta here." Everyone would be laughing, but I thought he was totally serious and I would be scared to death and I would cry. I went for years of really not liking him. I remember I was in a club and there was this man who said, "Hey, boy! What are you doing in here?" And he would continue until I cried. I didn't understand, and this would make me so afraid of adults and people of stature that are big. And I am intimidated by them because of that. They don't realize the pain that they are causing when they treat people like that. It's not funny.

  That's why, when I see children I am just the opposite. I am very, very kind, sensitive with them. I don't want to make any of those mistakes at all. My father used to do that to children. He doesn't anymore, but I remember when I was little [raises voice aggressively] . . . "What's your name? Where do you live?" and they would go [voice breaking], "I live down the street." I would go, "Why does he like making them cry? I'm sure it's very frightening." I have never forgotten that feeling, *ever*.

SB: But when you witness it, your reaction is, "I don't understand this. Why are you doing this?"

MJ: Why are you doing it? Why would you want to hurt someone like that? I can tell when a child is scared, you can see it in their eyes and hear it in their voice. Would you do something like that?

SB: I hope not. What made you hear him when even his own parents didn't hear him?

MJ: I can feel children, I can feel them. If they are hurting in any way I want to be there for them, wherever there is pain.

SB: You keep so much of this to yourself. You have, like, a poker face. When we go out to dinner, or when you come to our home, people are looking at you and thinking, "What is Michael thinking?" You keep this all inside.

MJ: Yeah. But, no, I feel it, I feel it so much. I can feel people's pain.

SB: Have you ever been embarrassed by anything? Children, of course, feel embarrassment.

MJ: Yes, I don't think you should embarrass children [by teasing them] unless they can laugh, too. I remember being embarrassed so badly. My father did it to me the worst. He would slap me as hard as he could and then push me out in front of my fans with tears rolling down my face. It's one thing to discipline, but you don't shame.

Security

*[Children] are more secure because...
their minds and their hearts and their
feelings are in the right place.*

SB: Children, at least initially, are utterly free of peer pressure. Of course, later, peer pressure becomes one of the hardest things in their lives. But when they're really young, they don't care what people think. Why don't they care what people think about them? We all care what people think about us. But kids don't care nearly as much. They're not image conscious until they grow older.

MJ: They are taught.

SB: Why do we care what other people think about us? Because we grow more insecure as we grow older, we want people to approve of us? Why are children more secure than adults?

MJ: Basically, they are more secure because they come from this G-dlike place, this other solar system where their minds and their hearts and their feelings are in the right place.

SB: So they are secure because they are connected to the source. And as you become more and more detached, we feel the light sort of diminish inside us and now we need other people to shine their light on us.

MJ: It's true. I have to guard myself sometimes because I see that sometimes I can inflict my feelings on Prince and Paris, because I am terrified of dogs and I feel bad that I was doing it to them, so I bought a golden retriever. People were like, "No, I can't believe you are doing this." I go, "I know, but they need it." Relatives, friends, my mother. They were shocked because there's this mantra about dogs. I don't want any because of my bad experience. That's one of the forms of racism and prejudice. But it would be wrong of me to alienate them in that way. I want them to find that out for themselves. I say to Prince, "We don't trust other people's dogs, but we trust this dog."

> *[Children] are secure because they are connected to the source. And as you become more and more detached, we feel the light sort of diminish inside us and now we need other people to shine their light on us.*

I've been to cases where a dog ate a girl's liver, they ate her lung, they bit the whole of a boy's side of his face so he's like this . . . Prince and Paris think they can walk up to any dog and go "Grrrr" to them. I said, "No, no, no, get back. Don't go 'Grrrr' to them."

SB: You decided that you didn't want to inflict your fears on the children.

MJ: That comes in not the dog and the child as a hypothesis or a test, but in so many other areas. We do this and we don't realize we are doing it. Parents need to search inside themselves and realize [raises voice] how *much* they are

World Children's Day and Family Dinners

*It would be the love of my life to have
a World Children's Day.*

SB: One of the things you told me you want to create is a World Children's Day, which would be an international day where all parents drop their work just to be with their children.

MJ: Children have no voice in society and they don't have a leader or anyone to speak for them and their rights, and to protect them, and that's the sad part, isn't it? It kills me. I couldn't gather up artists when this thing happened in Kosovo because people didn't care the way I cared. They say, "Yeah?" I said, "Don't you see what's happening with all these kids?" And they didn't care enough to want to do something. I didn't get that. I sat in my room and cried. I stopped recording my album for several days because I was so upset about it.

We want to make this a world holiday . . . worldwide, so we always take the day off. It can't be in the summer, it can't be a weekend. It will have to be a day where people stop and say, "Oh yes, we can't go to work tomorrow, or school tomorrow, because I have to be with my children and give them the whole uninterrupted day." It has to be like that or else it won't be important. It would be the love of my life to have a World Children's Day.

[The speech at Oxford] will be great because I can truly speak from my soul and say how I really feel about these issues. My dream is to have kids say, "It don't make no difference if you are black or white." I have always wanted to hear kids say that. Or "Heal the World." We didn't talk about [attaching a song with the day] that I could write and we could bring in all the celebrities, raise a lot of money, like a "We Are the World." But tie a song into it so in every country they are singing the same song, but in their language.

> *Children have no voice in society and they don't have a leader or anyone to speak for them and their rights, and to protect them.*

I want the holiday so badly, that's my dream. We should mention it to the UN. [Michael was pushing very hard at the time to become a United Nations Goodwill Ambassador for children. We had a number of meetings with some UN officials, but it did not materialize.] To me, it is criminal not to acknowledge the children. Our greatest asset . . . if there were children's day when I was little and I look at my father, "Okay, Daddy, Joseph, what are we going to do today?" Do you know what that would have meant for me? He'd go, "Well, do you want to go to the movies?" That would have meant so much to me. . . . You

just need that one moment of attention, I think, don't you think?

SB: Yes, absolutely.

MJ: I want that so badly, Shmuley. That's my dream.

SB: You know something. When we meet President Clinton tomorrow, we should tell him this. Imagine if we convinced President Clinton this should be the last great thing he does in his presidency? [Clinton, at the time, had six weeks left in office.] To simply try and establish—in addition to a Mother's Day and a Father's Day—a Child's

> We have to recognize that we have children and give them love. That would be so much for the future of those children and their parents and those children's children.

Day, where parents spend an uninterrupted day with their children. Clinton never knew his own father. This could be very meaningful to him.

MJ: That would be beautiful. I would love it, man.

SB: Now that you explained it to me, I understand it. You're right. Now parents will have their children come up to them and say, "Hey, Dad. It's my day. What are we doing?"

MJ: Yeah! And when they become adults, they would complete the circle and take care of their father and their mother, because of how they were treated when they were young. Come on, what's more beautiful than that? You

know, I think that's beautiful. We need to bring back family.

That's why I want kid's day, children's day, to do that. We have to recognize that we have children and give them love. That would be so much for the future of those children and their parents and those children's children. If I had a day like that with my father, our relationship would be totally different right now. I would have wonderful memories of when he took me to a park or toy store every time the children's day came, or to the movies. I just have that one memory of him placing me on that thing on that horse, on that pony.

SB: And you replay that memory a lot in your head?

MJ: It's all I have, I can't think of any other time. No games, no fun, nothing.

Michael pushed me hard to try to establish a World Children's Day. We went to the UN together, met a group of diplomats to try to make it happen, but it didn't.

I have, however, taken our joint vision of a regular, uninterrupted family time to launch an international family dinner night called Turn Friday Night into Family Night. Rather than giving kids only one day a year, it made sense that they deserved, at the very least, one day a week. Michael himself was a regular at our Friday night Sabbath meals, which he attended with Prince and Paris. He loved its peace, kinship, and restfulness.

You can help make this vision a reality. Go to www.fridayis family.com, where you can sign up. You'll see TV commercials with some of society's most respected personalities highlighting the initiative. It involves a simple commitment of giving you and your children the "Triple Two." Two uninterrupted hours with your children every Friday night, with two invited guests, to teach the kids sharing and hospitality, and discuss two important subjects, so you deepen their interest and enlighten their minds.

Making every Friday night family night will bring your family love, togetherness, and the blessing of the childlike spirit.

Coda
Sixteen Childlike Values for Adults, Parents, and Children

———— ◆◆◆ ————

Culled from my conversations with Michael in the previous chapters, here are reminders of the sixteen childlike virtues that help adults rediscover youthfulness, creativity, and innocence, as articulated by Michael.

CHERISHING, HONOR, AND RESPECT
"Thank you for making things so beautiful."

CHILDLIKE INNOCENCE
"Children are a reminder of . . . what we have to remember."

CREATIVITY AND INSPIRATION
"All [of the] most creative people act just like children."

CURIOSITY
"[Children] are fascinated by everything."

FORGIVENESS, FRIENDSHIP, AND LOYALTY
"Children fight, but they forgive each other in a second."

GIVING AND GENEROSITY
"I always had this yearning to give and help."

GRATITUDE AND THANKFULNESS
"I can't take credit for everything I do. . . .
There is always some higher source."

HOPE AND THE DIVINE
"[Children] are G-d's way of saying there is hope,
there is such a thing as humanity."

HUMOR, PLAY, AND LAUGHTER
"Just let go and be free-spirited."

IMAGINATION
"Our minds create our world."

JEALOUSY, ENVY, AND ADMIRATION
"Never jealous . . . complete admiration. . . .
Complete inspiration, never jealousy."

JOY
"Children come with the quintessence of bliss."

LOVE AND GUIDANCE
"You can't overdose on love."

OPENNESS AND VULNERABILITY
"I love how a child is so honest."

SECURITY
"[Children] are more secure because . . . their minds and their hearts and their feelings are in the right place."

WORLD CHILDREN'S DAY AND FAMILY DINNERS
"It would be the love of my life to have a World Children's Day."
Go to www.fridayisfamily.com, and sign up.

Acknowledgments

Michael Jackson died much too young. For many, he will live on through his dance and music. For me, he will live through the warm friendship we shared and powerful words contained in this and the previous volume of our conversations, *The Michael Jackson Tapes*. I thank him for his candor, courage, and honesty in sharing so much of himself with a public that he knew was suspicious of him. Yet Michael took a leap of faith in recording these conversations for publication in the belief that he could go beyond people's cynicism and open their hearts to the childhood spirit. In so doing, he believed he could make the world softer, kinder, and gentler.

This is a book about the wonders of childhood. My own children—Mushki, Chana, Shterny, Mendy, Shaina, Rochel Leah, Yosef, Dovid Chaim, and Cheftziba—are most responsible for whatever childlike awe I have retained. They are the light, they are the joy, of my life.

The same applies to Prince and Paris Jackson, who were my children's playmates when they were young, and Blanket, whom we never met. I will never forget how much your father loved you. I think of you often and ask that G-d protect you and keep you. In the words of Joseph to Benjamin, recorded in the Bible, "May G-d be gracious to you, my child."

Francesco Cascio, Michael's former manager and close friend, was instrumental in making sure that Michael and I got together regularly to record these sessions for the publication of these books. I thank Frank for more than a decade of continued and living friendship.

Janet Goldstein expertly edited and arranged my conversations with Michael and helped to present them in an accessible, inspirational, and well-ordered manner. She has my gratitude and deep thanks.

Roger Cooper, the publisher at Vanguard, is a man of courage, determination, humanity, and vision. Without him, neither of the Michael Jackson books that are based on our conversations would have seen the light of day.

My wife, Debbie, is the principal blessing of my life and my alter ego in all things. I do nothing of consequence without first seeking her counsel and guidance, and feel lost when she is not beside me.

My parents, Yoav Botach and Eleanor Paul, imparted to me not just unconditional love but my deepest values and the belief that I always had something positive to contribute.

My siblings, Sara, Bar Kochva, Chaim Moshe, and Ateret, are my closest friends and confidants.

Shneur Zalman Fellig inspired me from a young age to deepen my relationship with Judaism and G-d. It was his early influence that set me on the road to becoming a rabbi and devoting my life to teaching values.

Rabbi Menachem Schneerson, the Lubavitcher Rebbe, of blessed memory, remains, even sixteen years after his death, the person who most shaped my spirituality, humanity, and communal commitment. The good that is in me was in no small measure unearthed through witnessing his tireless commitment to countless thousands in need. I miss my Rebbe every day.

G-d Almighty has always shone His light and grace on me, notwithstanding how undeserving I have been. Thank you, Lord, for the beauty of my children and the devotion of my wife, for the comfort of human friendship, and for always walking with me and illuminating my path.

Finally, to the children of the world, thank you for making us stodgy, irritable adults a little bit younger, a little bit more open, and so much more happy. G-d bless you all.

Honoring
the
Child Spirit